国家智库报告 2016（26）
National Think Tank

学 术 评 价

全球智库评价报告
（2015）

荆林波 等著

GLOBAL THINK TANK EVALUATION REPORT（2015）

中国社会科学出版社

图书在版编目（CIP）数据

全球智库评价报告（2015）／荆林波等著 . —北京：中国社会科学出版社，
2016.7
（国家智库报告）
ISBN 978 - 7 - 5161 - 8675 - 6

Ⅰ.①全…　Ⅱ.①荆…　Ⅲ.①咨询机构—研究报告—世界
Ⅳ.①C932.81

中国版本图书馆 CIP 数据核字（2016）第 178645 号

出 版 人	赵剑英
责任编辑	王　茵
特约编辑	范晨星
责任校对	石春梅
责任印制	李寡寡

出　　　版	中国社会科学出版社
社　　　址	北京鼓楼西大街甲 158 号
邮　　　编	100720
网　　　址	http://www.csspw.cn
发 行 部	010 - 84083685
门 市 部	010 - 84029450
经　　　销	新华书店及其他书店

印刷装订	北京君升印刷有限公司
版　　　次	2016 年 7 月第 1 版
印　　　次	2016 年 7 月第 1 次印刷

开　　　本	787×1092　1/16
印　　　张	13
插　　　页	2
字　　　数	140 千字
定　　　价	56.00 元

课题主持人： 荆林波

课题组成员： 吴　敏　　姜庆国

刘潇潇　　胡　薇　　杨卓颖　　沈进建

马　冉　　刘冰洁　　王力力　　苏金燕

逯万辉　　耿海英　　余　倩　　郝若扬

杨发庭　　相均泳　　张青松　　徐璟毅

郝　明　　李　军　　吴　波　　邹青山

陈媛媛　　冯守礼　　侯轶雄　　何玉琼

王春红　　李钰莹　　索建次　　陈　瑶

卢珊珊　　章　璋　　王利民　　周　群

李文珍　　姚晓丹　　王　萍　　刘华初

杨　雪　　薛晓莹　　张小溪　　褚国飞

南英舜

数据采集人员： 杨　敏　　张　琳　　邵雅楠　　韩　旭

曹元元　　胡　纯　　林志威　　李　硕

王秀中　　郑步高　　于嘉莹

目　　录

一　智库的界定

智库（think tank），过去多被翻译成"思想库"，就是各种智囊机构，又被称作"思想工厂"（think factory）、"外脑"（outside brain）、"脑库"（brain tank）、"智囊团"（brain trust）、"咨询公司"（consultant corporation）或"情报研究中心"（intelligence research center），等等。

最初，它是第二次世界大战期间美国为国防科学家和军事参谋提供的一种能够让他们在一起讨论战略问题的密室。

《世界知识大辞典》将"思想库"定义为："思想库又称脑库、智囊团。一种为政府机关、企业、公司、社团提供研究咨询的智力劳动集团，一般由多学科、多专业的专家组成"。①

《大英百科全书》认为：智库是跨学科研究组织的研究所、公司或者团体，通常为政府和商业客户服务。

---

① 安国政等：《世界知识大辞典》，世界知识出版社 1990 年版，第 1356 页。

保罗·迪克森在 1971 年出版了第一部介绍美国智库形成与发展的专著——《智库》，他提出：智库是"独立的、非营利的政策研究机构"，它是一个永久性的实体，而非临时为解决问题而组成的研究小组或委员会，其目的是为政策而非技术服务。①

詹姆斯·史密斯认为：智库是"在美国主流政治进程的边缘运行的、私人的、非营利的研究型团体，介于社会科学学术研究和高等教育之间，以及政府和党派政治之间"。②

耶鲁大学政治学博士安德鲁·里奇认为：智库是"独立的、没有利益倾向的非营利性组织，它们提供专业知识或建议，并以此获得支持，影响决策过程"。③

加拿大思想库研究专家唐纳德·E. 埃布尔森认为，智库是"由关心广泛公共政策问题的人组成的独立的、非营利性的组织"。④

---

① Paul Dickson, *Think Tank*, New York：Atheneum, 1971.

② James A. Smith, *The Idea Brokers：Think Tanks and the Rise of the New Policy Elite*, New York：The Free Press, 1993, p. XIII.

③ Andrew Rich, "US Think Tank and The Intersection of Ideology Advocacy and Influence", *NIRA Review*, Winter 2001, p. 54.

④ Donald E. Abelson, *American Think Tanks and their Role in US Foreign Policy*, New York：St. Martin's Press, 1996, p. 21.

在我国，对于"思想库"与"智囊团"存在着不同的认识。

根据百度百科的解释：智库即智囊机构，最初也称"思想库"，是指由专家组成的、多学科的、为决策者在处理社会、经济、科技、军事、外交等各方面问题出谋划策，提供最佳理论、策略、方法、思想等的公共研究机构。严格意义上的智库是独立于政府机构的民间组织。智库的主要职能是：提出思想、教育公众和会集人才。智库首先通过研究和分析形成新的政策主张，再通过出版书刊、举办各类交流活动、利用媒体宣传等方式，力图使这些主张获得公众的支持和决策者的青睐。

有的学者认为"思想库"是指人们在社会实践中产生的理性认识（思想）的储备集合体；而"智囊团"则是指足智多谋、议政参政的群体。[①]

总之，如何定义智库已经成为一个长期困扰我们的问题。我们很难给这些种类不同的组织找到一个统一的定义，这很大程度上是因为人们对怎样才算是一个智库众说纷纭。苦苦探讨智库的定义之后，大多数学者终于

---

① 陈振声：《中国社科院真正成为中央思想库和智囊团的思考》，载张冠梓主编《国情调研（2006）》，山东人民出版社 2008 年版，第 845 页。

承认，根本不存在统一模式的智库。① 尽管如此，加拿大学者唐纳德·E. 埃布尔森认为智库的运作方式类似私人企业，但其最终效益不是以利润来衡量，而是看它们对政策思想的影响。美国和加拿大的智库分别根据《所得税法》（*Income Tax Act*）和《国内税收法》（*Internal Revenue Code*）注册为非营利的免税组织。为了获得免税资格，它们不得支持任何政治派别。智库与政策制定共同体中的其他各种组织之间的一个传统区别是，智库强调研究和分析。②

综上所述，我们认为，智库就是通过自主的知识产品对公共政策的制定产生影响的组织。我们对智库概念的界定强调：

首先，智库是一个组织，不是自然人，这是智库的组织要件。智库活动有别于个人行为，中国历史上的"诸葛亮""刘伯温"等个人谋士无法构成智库。

其次，智库必须有自主的知识产品。智库是专业化的知识制造者，需要具备专业知识技能的人员来开发创

---

① ［加］唐纳德·E. 埃布尔森：《智库能发挥作用吗?》，扈喜林译，上海社会科学院出版社 2010 年版，第 5—6 页。

② 博鳌论坛研讨会会议纪要：《智库在决策中的作用》，2015 年 3 月 29 日。

造新的思想产品。

最后，智库要对公共政策的制定产生影响，这是智库的核心功能。我们认为，智库对公共政策具有影响力，并不一定要被理解为具有特殊的政治意识形态倾向。正如兰德公司就不愿意给自己贴上"智库"的标签，在其官方网站上对此有特别说明：鉴于目前"智库"被理解为具有特殊的政治或思想意识形态倾向的组织，故兰德公司不再使用"智库"标签。兰德公司始终强调：兰德的"核心价值观是质量和客观，注重的是事实与证据"。

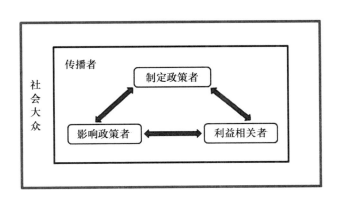

图1 智库的社会网络结构

资料来源：课题组绘制。

制定政策者、影响政策者和利益相关者之间进行着不断的沟通，利益相关者试图直接影响政策制定者的决策，或者间接地通过影响政策者对政策制定者施压，获得对自身有利的政策的出台。

二 智库评价方法的对比分析

对于智库的评价，可谓仁者见仁，智者见智。

国外学者在评估智库的影响力方面，做了许多尝试。其中的一种方法是对智库业绩进行定量评估，计算它们带来了多少媒体报道、员工向立法委员会陈述观点的次数。[1]

安德鲁·里奇和肯特·威佛仔细分析了美国51家智库的知名度，发现被媒体报道数量多的机构比媒体形象一般的智库更有可能被召集到国会，向国会陈述观点。[2]

安德鲁·里奇在另外的研究中发现，那些媒体报道数量多的智库与那些被政策制定者和其他意见领袖认为是最有影响的智库之间似乎存在某种关系。[3]

之后，唐纳德·E.埃布尔森对比研究了美国和加拿

---

① ［加］唐纳德·E．埃布尔森：《智库能发挥作用吗?》，第89页。

② Andrew Rich and R. Kent Weaver, "Think Tanks, the Media and the Policy Process", Paper presented at the 1997 annual meeting of the American Political Science Association, Washington, D. C., August 1997.

③ Andrew Rich, "Perceptions of Think Tanks in American Politics: A Survey of Congressional Staff and Journalists," Burson-Marstellar Worldwide Report, December 1997.

大两国智库影响政策制定的机遇、制约因素和有利条件，分析了公众知名度和政策的相关性。

我国学者也对智库的影响力做了探索。比如，朱旭峰对中国思想库影响力进行了实证分析，[①] 还有一些学者与机构进行了相关尝试。

从目前国内外的智库评价情况来看，主要有三个智库评价项目受到较多的关注与热议。

（一） 美国宾夕法尼亚大学的《全球智库报告》

美国宾夕法尼亚大学所属的"智库与市民社会项目（TTCSP）"课题组（以下简称为"项目组"）从 2006 年开始，探索全球智库的评价机制，并逐步形成了其特有的一套智库评价流程。具体而言，首先，在每年春季向其项目资料库中的人员以及其他感兴趣的公众发送邮件，邀请他们登录项目组网站，并推荐有资格参加"国际咨询委员会"（International Advisory Committee，以下简称为 IAC）的人员名单及联系方式。然后，项目组向 IAC 成员发出提名邀请，请他们按照若干类别分别提名每个

---

① 朱旭峰：《中国思想库：政策过程中的影响力研究》，清华大学出版社 2009 年版。

类别中他们认为能够排在前 25 名的智库。在汇总提名结果后，将所有被提名为顶级智库的候选机构的汇总资料发给"专家小组"（Expert Panelists，以下简称为 EP 成员），邀请他们参考项目组提供的评价指标对这些经过筛选的机构进行分类排名、确认和调整，在每年年底确定各个类别的最终排名。

表 1　　　　　　　　　　《全球智库报告》的智库评价指标体系

评价方面	具体特征
资源指标	吸引与保留领先学者和分析家的能力 财务支持水平、质量和稳定性 与政策制定者和其他政策精英的关系 人员从事严谨研究、提供及时和精准分析的能力 机构的筹资能力 网络的质量和可靠性 在政策学术界的重点联系及其与媒体的关系
效用指标	在该国媒体和政治精英中的声誉 媒体曝光与被引用数量和质量 网站的点击率 提交给立法和行政机构的专家证词的数量和质量 政府部门的简报 政府任命 书籍的销售量 研究报告的传播情况 在学术刊物与大众出版物上的被引用情况 举办会议的参加情况 组织的研讨会

续表

评价方面	具体特征
产出指标	政策建议与创新理念的数量与质量 出版物（包括图书、期刊文章、政策简报等）的状况 新闻访谈情况 会议和研讨会的组织情况 所属人员被任命为顾问或到政府部门任职的情况
影响力指标	政策建议被决策者和社会组织采纳的情况 网络的聚焦状况 在政党、竞选人、过渡团队中起到的咨询作用 获得的荣誉 在学术期刊、公共证词和媒体关注的政策辩论会上的成果 列表和网站的优势 挑战传统智慧的成功 在政府运行和民选官员中的作用

资料来源：课题组根据相关资料汇总归纳。参见 ［美］詹姆斯·G. 麦甘《2013 年全球智库报告》，上海社会科学院出版社 2014 年版。

根据介绍，项目组在 2011 年度共向全球 182 个国家的 6545 家智库发出了参评邀请，并收到了 120 个国家的 1500 多位个人的提名回复。其后项目组要求提名者按照 30 个类别分别推荐出各类别中排在前 25 名的智库，30 个类别共收到 25000 项提名，被提名智库共计 5329 家，其中 202 家智库被提名为世界顶级智库。[①]

美国宾夕法尼亚大学"智库与市民社会项目"

---

① 王继承：《麦甘"全球智库报告"排名机制及其影响》，《中国经济时报》2012 年 8 月 28 日。

（TTCSP）课题组较早地开始了对全球智库的评价和排名研究，并将该项目持续推进至今，已取得了智库研究领域的一项标杆性成果。该项目采用的是整体性测度方法中的"主观整体印象评价法"，此方法简便易行，因此尽管该项目组中只有詹姆斯·G.麦甘（以下简称为"麦甘"）一名专职工作人员，但也可以通过实习学生的帮助顺利完成每年的问卷调查工作。

然而，《全球智库报告》在得到多方肯定的同时，不可否认，该报告也存在着诸多问题。在对历年的《全球智库报告》加以系统研究分析之后，我们认为该报告主要存在如下六大问题。

第一，评价方法欠缺客观性，有待进一步完善。在全球智库排名工作中，麦甘采用的是"主观整体印象评价法"。这种评价方法的优点是简便易行，可以快速地对大量客观主体（比如全球智库）进行评价。但与此同时，这种评价方法的缺点也十分明显，具体而言就是主观导向的影响过大，评价者所处的地域、所研究的领域、所持有的观点等都会对全球智库的评价产生不同程度的影响，因而也必然会影响到全球智库评价结果的准确性。我们认为，客观且全面的全球智库评价方法不仅要有主观的评价，而且更需要有大量的、多层次的客观指标的评价。只有主观定性评价与客观定量评价相结合，才能较为全面地对全球智库作出相对公正客观的评价。

第二，研究力量有待充实。很显然，承担全球智库评价如此庞大的项目，必须拥有一支具备科学素养的研究团队，必须有相对稳定的财力支持。尤其是，麦甘所采用的"主观整体印象评价法"要求必须通过优秀的调研人员来最大限度地去除主观评价中的偏差，这是保证"主观整体印象评价法"有效实施的关键环节。然而，非常遗憾的是，麦甘所进行的该评价项目只由他一名全职工作人员负责，而这个项目的数据收集、研究和分析，不是借助于实地调研或者专业的工作人员进行的，而是依靠来自宾夕法尼亚大学和费城地区其他高校的实习学生进行的。我们在海外实地调研中曾经见到了参加全球智库评价项目的实习学生，这些学生本身没有经过严格的学术训练，对于全球智库的理解也比较粗浅，有的学生只是把该项目作为暑期实习以获得调研经历而已，由此可见依靠实习生进行的调研，其调研质量是令人担忧的。

第三，专家遴选机制有待规范化与透明化。从麦甘发布的报告可以看出，该排名工作中最重要的一环是专家小组的形成。2011年，麦甘通过在互联网平台上公开民主推荐国际咨询委员会（IAC）和专家小组（EP成员）的方式，吸收来自各地区和各研究领域的专家小组成员、跨领域的记者与学者、现任和前任智库负责人、智库的捐助人、社会民众的代表以及其他智库相关人员等组成了专家小组。然而，麦甘并没有给出专家小组成员的专业领域、地区所属、职务职称等具体分布情况，例如亚洲地区有多少人员参与到国际咨询委员会和专家小组等，这些专家成员的构成会直接影响到调查样本对该地区智库的认知熟悉程度。在麦甘致专家小组成员的一封电子邮件中，他明确告诉这些评选专家，"你的选择和排名将被严加保密"，同时，麦甘还向评选专家提议，"如果你没有时间为所有智库排名，那就花上几分钟为你所在的地区或你的专业领域的智库排一下名"。这种随意的评选要求显示出该项目在质量把控方面太过宽松草率。

第四，报告存在较多漏洞，难以令人信服，有许多值得商榷的地方。比如，2009年将"麻省理工大学经济系"单独拿出来排在"科学和技术类前10"中的第2名，而在此后历年的系列报告中，该智库再也没有在这一类别里出现。欧洲学者早在2010年就系统地整理出部分西欧智库在该报告排名榜上所存在的自相矛盾之处，例如英国的"大赦国际"在"西欧前40"中只排到第12名，却同时又被排在了"世界前10（非美国）"中的第5名；在"西欧前40"中比大赦国际排名还要靠前的德国"艾伯特基金会"却未排进"世界前10（非美国）"类别之中等，不一致的地方多达20余处。再比如，2012年的报告将中国社会科学院下属的"世界经济与政治研究所"单独拿出来与中国社会科学院一起参与排名，显然没有搞清楚机构之间的隶属关系。

第五，工作态度不够严谨。例如，2010年该项目组在短短10天之内就公开发布了三个不同版本的报告（即1月21日、25日、31日）。对此，有学者指出在第一个版本中，智利的"拉丁美洲和加勒比海经济委员会"被排在拉丁美洲和加勒比海地区的第一名，而在另外两个版本中，这一机构再也没有出现在前40名之中，此外还出现了一个机构在同一张表格中被同时排出两个不同名次的错误。类似的错误也出现在《2014年全球智库报告》中，在该报告的"世界顶级智库（含美国）"150强榜单里，排在第48名与第99名的智库都是中国的"国务院发展研究中心"，如此大的错误，足见其工作态度的粗疏。更令人困惑不解的是"布鲁金斯学会"在2012年"环境类前70"排名中位列第2名，然而布鲁金斯学会却在其官方网站上公开声明其并不关注环境政策方面的研究。类似的现象连续出现了几年，即布鲁金斯学会在多个分类排名中都被排入了前10名，而不管他们是否在该领域有研究活动。

第六，《全球智库报告》尚未取得全球范围的普遍认可，其新闻通稿的宣传内容存在不实之处。2015年新闻通稿中宣称，"《全球智库报告》是在数千名国际专家学者的提名基础上，依据科学系统的标准而形成的评定结果，自2007年发布全球智库排名至今，已逐渐成为反映全球智库表现和综合影响力的国际风向标"。而我们在对美国多家著名智库进行调研时发现，大家的看法并非如此。当然，布鲁金斯学会很乐意见到自己被该报告评为"全球第一智库"，并且在其官方网站上对此进行大张旗鼓的宣传。然而我们到美国其他智库调研时，无论是美国卡内基和平基金会、美国企业研究所，还是美国战略与国际研究中心、美国外交关系委员会，抑或传统基金会、世界资源研究所，它们都对布鲁金斯学会荣膺"全球第一智库"不以为然。只有在自己被报告的某个分类评为第一时，他们才会接受其评价结果。

综上所述，我们认为，《全球智库报告》目前还存在诸多问题，其权威性也受到多方的质疑。对此，国内很多媒体并没能做到全面而客观地加以报道，以致出现了一些学者、研究机构和媒体在不明事实的情况下，盲目跟风炒作的现象。我们建议对此类研究报告必须慎重对待、严加甄别，不可过高评估其价值。

（二）上海社会科学院的《中国智库报告》

2014 年 1 月 22 日，上海社会科学院智库研究中心发布了中国第一份《中国智库报告》，并公布了中国智库影响力排名，其排行榜分综合影响力排名、系统影响力排名和专业影响力排名三大类。该项目的评价方法基本上是参考麦甘的"主观整体印象评价法"，对我国智库的评价主要考核了四个方面，具体参见表 2。

表 2　　　　　　　　　　　中国智库影响力评价标准

评价方面	具体特征
智库成长与营销能力	智库成立时间与存续时间长短 智库的研究经费投入 留住顶级专家和研究者的能力 与国内外同类机构合作交流的渠道
决策（核心）影响力	智库研究成果荣获领导批示次数及层次 智库专家参与决策咨询的次数及层次 智库专家应邀给决策者授课的次数及层次 智库专家到政府部门中的任职比例以及智库人员曾在政府部门任职的比例（"旋转门"机制）
学术（中心）影响力	智库人员在国内外核心期刊发表、被转载的论文数量 智库人员应邀参加国内外学术会议的数量及层次 公开出版学术专著、会议论文集等出版物 公开出版连续型研究报告
公众（边缘）影响力	智库专家在媒体上发表成果或被媒体报道的频率 智库学者接受媒体采访的频率 智库网站建设，包括智库专家拥有博客、微博等自媒体的数量 智库研究对社会弱势群体政策需求的人文关怀

　　资料来源：上海社会科学院智库研究中心：《2013 年中国智库报告——影响力排名与政策建议》，上海社会科学院出版社 2014 年版。

　　2015 年，上海社会科学院智库研究中心对智库评价的体系进行了修改，围绕中国智库的决策咨询影响力、学术影响力、媒体影响力、公众影响力、国际影响力，以及智库成长与营销能力设定评价标准，采用多轮主观评价方法，就中国活跃智库的综合影响力、分项影响力、系统内部的影响力和专业影响力等方面进行打分与排名，并在此基础上，总结归纳了中国最具影响力智库的主要特征。具体评价标准参见表3。

表3   中国智库影响力评价标准

评价方面	具体特征
决策影响力	智库研究成果荣获各级领导批示 智库专家参与决策咨询或给决策者授课的次数及层次 智库专家到政府部门中的任职比例以及智库人员曾在政府部门任职的比例（"旋转门"机制）
学术影响力	智库人员在国内外核心期刊发表、转载的论文数量 智库人员应邀参加国内外学术会议的数量及层次 公开出版学术专著、会议论文集和连续型研究报告等
媒体影响力	智库对媒体舆论的引导能力 智库专家接受媒体采访、报道或在媒体上发表成果的频率 智库网站建设，包括智库专家拥有博客、微博等自媒体的数量
公众影响力	智库对公众意识的引导能力 智库研究对社会弱势群体政策需求的关注关怀与行动效果
国际影响力	国际知名度、国际声誉 与国外同类机构合作交流的频率 对国际重大事件的持续关注与分析能力
智库成长与营销能力	智库成立时间与存续有较长的历史时期 智库的研究经费投入 留住顶级专家和精英学者的能力

资料来源：上海社会科学院智库研究中心：《2014年中国智库报告——影响力排名与政策建议》，上海社会科学院出版社2015年版。

　　上海社会科学院智库研究中心认为：智库影响力是其决策影响力、学术影响力、媒体影响力、公众影响力和国际影响力的综合体现，加上智库影响力实现的一整套渠道和机制，即智库的成长与营销能力等，共同构成报告对于中国智库影响力的评价标准。同时，考虑到影响力是一种主观评价，往往因人、因事而异，很难用具体的指标加以测量。为此，项目组以多轮主观评价法为主，利用相对模糊的序数排名，参考个别定量指标，对智库影响力进行评价。

　　上海社会科学院开创了我国智库评价的先河，最早推出了有关智库评价的报告，明确提出了自己的评价智库影响力的指标体系。

　　上海社会科学院对中国智库进行了分类分析，即把中国智库划分为党政军智库、社会科学院智库、高校智库和民间智库四大类，并且对它们各自的智库性质、组织形态、经费来源和研究方向等进行了对比分析。[①]

　　值得一提的是，上海社会科学院根据中国智库分类演化与研究领域的特点，在 2013 年的报告中设计了三类

---

　　① 　上海社会科学院智库研究中心：《2013 年中国智库报告——影响力排名与政策建议》，上海社会科学院出版社 2014 年版，第 9 页。

排名：第一类综合影响力排名，第二类系统影响力排名，第三类专业影响力排名。

上海社会科学院的中国智库报告中存在的问题，主要体现在：

第一，对智库的界定有待进一步明确。正如报告所言：目前对高校智库的遴选，在综合影响力和系统影响力的评选时，以所在大学为单位；在专业影响力评选时，以高校下属的二级学院和研究中心为单位。如何界定高校智库，将涉及智库数量和规模等问题，值得进一步探讨。①

第二，评价方法有待完善。这是一个比较关键的问题。上海社会科学院目前采用的是"提名＋评选＋排名"的主观评价方法，应当逐步改用"主观＋客观"的评价方法。②

当然，更重要的是评价程序的透明度，评价权重的设定。比如，哪些人参与了问卷调研，评委专家的构成、地域分布、学科分布是否均衡等，这些对最终的评价结

---

① 上海社会科学院智库研究中心：《2013 年中国智库报告——影响力排名与政策建议》，上海社会科学院出版社 2014 年版，第 43 页。

② 同上书，第 42—43 页。

果起着至关重要的作用，应当公开相关信息。再比如，即使采取主观评价方法，也应当对评价指标的权重加以说明，特别是对排名榜单中的相关智库的得分给予披露，让被评智库做到清楚明了，知道自己赢在哪里，输在哪里。而现在只是一个简单的排行榜，无法起到让相关智库发现差距的作用，也很难让他人对其评价工作进行合理的衡量和评判。

（三）零点国际发展研究院与中国网的智库评价

2015 年 1 月 15 日，零点国际发展研究院与中国网联合发布了《2014 中国智库影响力报告》。根据该智库影响力分类，采用四类影响力指标：专业影响力、政府影响力、社会影响力和国际影响力。每类影响力设置 3—5 个客观指标，如表 4 所示：

表 4　　　　　　　　　中国智库影响力评价指标

评价指标	具体指标
专业影响力	智库研究人才的数量和国际化程度 智库主要研究人员在期刊上发表文章的数量 智库主要研究人员出版专著的数量 智库公开发行刊物的数量

续表

评价指标	具体指标
政府影响力	智库为政府人员培训的数量和级别 智库承担政府委托项目的数量和级别 智库获得政府领导批示的数量和级别 智库参加政府部门座谈会的数量和级别
社会影响力	智库在互联网搜索引擎上的搜索量 国内主流媒体对智库的报道量 智库及其主要负责人在新媒体上的粉丝量
国际影响力	智库与国际机构合作的频次和方式 与智库合作的国外智库的数量 智库主要研究人员在国际论坛上发言的数量 国外媒体对智库的报道量 智库在国外设立分支机构的数量

资料来源：零点国际发展研究院与中国网：《2014中国智库影响力报告》，2015年1月15日。

每个二级指标在数据收集过程中可能会根据实际情况再分为更详细的指标，比如研究人员数量会再细分为国内研究人员和国外研究人员。

为了保证研究结果更加客观，零点国际发展研究院与中国网将上海社会科学院的排名作为一级指标，将排名换算为得分后，与他们通过客观指标加总得到的分值进行综合后计算出智库的最终得分，即采用如下公式：

$$智库得分 = 客观指标得分 \times 70\% + 主观指数得分 \times 30\%$$

从公式可知，智库排名的得分以量化的客观指标为主。零点国际发展研究院与中国网期望建立一套完全由量化指标构成的体系，但这一体系的确立还需要多年的积累和试错。主观得分的比重将在以后逐年减小，直至去除。

就零点国际发展研究院与中国网的《2014 中国智库影响力报告》而言，首先，其评价智库的运作模式有所创新，评价机构来自民间研究机构与媒体合作研究是一大亮点。其次，他们试图改进评价方法，创造出主观评价与客观评价相结合的评价方法，并且尝试把上海社会科学院的评价结果作为来源数据，但与此同时，他们也同样没有公开相关智库的最后得分，也没有完全展示量化的过程，缺乏评价的透明度。尤其是对智库的界定没有给出一个明确的范围，对智库的客观数据、打分等也没有加以公开。我们在调研中与零点国际发展研究院的相关人员进行了交流，他们也认为数据的采集仍然存在较大的问题，对数据采集所投入的人员和时间不够充足，评价过程中征求的专家也还不够全面。

三　全球智库综合评价 AMI 指标体系

全球智库综合评价指标体系主要从吸引力、管理力和影响力三个层次对全球智库进行评价，具体评价模型如图 2 所示。

吸引力（Attractive Power）：指全球智库的外部环境，良好的外部环境能够吸引更多的资源，提升评价客体的吸引力。

管理力（Management Power）：指全球智库的管理者管理评价客体的能力和促进评价客体发展的能力。

影响力（Impact Power）：是全球智库的直接表现，是吸引力和管理力水平的最终体现。

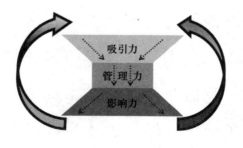

图 2　全球智库综合评价模型

资料来源：课题组绘制。

（一） 全球智库综合评价指标体系

综合评价指标体系由五级指标构成，总分值为 355 分，其中一级指标"吸引力"的分值为 105 分，"管理力"的分值为 70 分，"影响力"的分值为 180 分。

表5　　　　　　　　　全球智库综合评价指标体系

一级指标	二级指标	三级指标	四级指标	五级指标
吸引力	声誉吸引力	决策奖励	机构或其工作人员获得国际或国家级别政府、行业、组织的奖励	
		学术声誉	机构或其工作人员报告、论文、著作等获得国家级奖励	
			研究人员学术道德	
			学术独立性	研究方向和研究内容独立性
				研究结论独立性
		历史	成立时间	
		同行评议	专家评估	
			第三方评估	
	人员吸引力	人员规模	工作人员总数	
		求职比		
		吸引人才的能力	工作环境	
			提供平台	
			个人职业规划	
			待遇	专职工作人员税后平均年收入

续表

一级指标	二级指标	三级指标	四级指标	五级指标
吸引力	产品/成果吸引力	研究成果吸引力	论文下载量	
			论文转载量	
			网站点击量	网站年点击量
	资金吸引力	资金值	人均年研发经费	
		资金来源	多元化	
管理力	战略	发展规划		
	组织	组织层次	严密性、系统性	
		独立性	独立法人资格	
		客户关系管理	与政府、学术机构、媒体、企业、国外机构的关系	专职公关人员
	系统	信息化管理	独立网站	
		流程管理	规章制度	建立与执行的规范性
			战略战术	协调性
		外包能力	翻译	
			数据处理	
			社会调查	
	人员	素质	工作人员学历	拥有学士学位的工作人员数量占工作人员总数的比例
		结构	年龄结构	30—50岁工作人员占全体工作人员的比例
			性别结构	两性专业技术人员数量差与全体专业技术人员数量的比例
		领导人	管理能力	
		合作能力		
	风格	管理风格	历史传统，文化传承	
	价值观	导向管理	明确的价值观和使命感	
	技术	专业技术能力	专业技术人员学历	
			分析决策水平	

一级指标	二级指标	三级指标	四级指标	五级指标
影响力	政策影响力	对政策制定的影响力	政府委托研究项目	数量
			研究人员受邀为省部级及以上政府授课、接受省部级及以上政府咨询	人次
			成果对政策的影响力	决策采纳率
		与政府及决策者的关系	旋转门	曾经在省部级政府任职（包括挂职）的工作人员数量占工作人员总数的比例
				离开机构到省部级政府任职的工作人员数量占工作人员总数的比例
				在省部级政府兼职的工作人员数量占工作人员总数的比例
				曾任省部级及以上政府官员的工作人员数量占工作人员总数的比例
				离开机构任省部级及以上政府官员的工作人员数量占工作人员总数的比例
			官员培训	
	学术影响力	成果发布	出版连续出版物	数量
			发布研究报告、发表学术论文、出版学术著作	专业技术人员公开发布研究报告、发表学术论文的数量
				专业技术人员提交非公开研究报告的数量
				专业技术人员出版学术著作的数量
		论文被引	论文被引量	专业技术人员学术论文被引总量
		学术活动活跃度	举办会议	单独或联合举办公开学术研讨会、圆桌会议、论坛的次数
			学术交流	与国内其他学术机构互访总次数

一级指标	二级指标	三级指标	四级指标	五级指标
影响力	社会影响力	媒体曝光度	人员媒体曝光度	专业技术人员在国家级广播、电视、报纸和网络媒体发表政策性观点的总次数
			机构媒体曝光度	机构获得国家级广播、电视、报纸、网络媒体报道（含转载）的总次数
		社会责任	社会公益项目	开展社会公益项目的数量
		信息公开度	研究成果开放获取	
			网站内容	丰富性
			网站更新频率	
			成果推送	
	国际影响力	国际合作	与国外机构联合举办学术研讨会、圆桌会议、论坛的总次数	
			与国外机构或个人合作发布学术成果总件数	
			派往国外进行学术访问，参与学术交流、研讨会的总人次	
		注册国外分支机构	数量	
		外籍专业技术人员	外籍专业技术人员数量占专业技术人员总数的比例	
		使用多语种	专业技术人员公开发布研究报告、发表学术论文使用语言	总数
			机构网站语言版本	数量

（二）全球智库综合评价指标体系（2015 年试用版）

在对全球智库进行评价之际，为了进一步检验"全球智库综合评价指标体系"的科学性与适用性，特制定了"全球智库综合评价指标体系（2015 年试用版）"（以下简称为"评价指标体系 2015 试用版"）。此次，我们基于指标获取性及时间紧迫性等原因，从全球智库综合评价指标体系的子类之中选取了其中的大部分指标作为评价指标体系 2015 试用版的指标，并以此对全球智库进行评价。

评价指标体系 2015 试用版的一级指标"吸引力"的分值为 82 分，"管理力"的分值为 51 分，"影响力"的分值为 150 分，总分值为 283 分，与完整版评价指标体系相比，总分值减少 72 分（见表 6）。

表6　　　　　　全球智库综合评价指标体系（2015 年试用版）

一级指标	二级指标	三级指标	四级指标	五级指标
吸引力	声誉吸引力	学术声誉	学术独立性	研究方向和研究内容独立性
				研究结论独立性
		历史	成立时间	
		同行评议	专家评估	
			第三方评估	

续表

一级指标	二级指标	三级指标	四级指标	五级指标
吸引力	人员吸引力	人员规模	工作人员总数	
		求职比		
		吸引人才的能力	待遇	专职工作人员税后平均年收入
	产品/成果吸引力	研究成果吸引力	网站点击量	网站年点击量
	资金吸引力	资金值	人均年研发经费	
		资金来源	多元化	
管理力	战略	发展规划		
	组织	独立性	独立法人资格	
		客户关系管理	与政府、学术机构、媒体、企业、国外机构的关系	专职公关人员
	系统	信息化管理	独立网站	
		外包能力	翻译	
			数据处理	
			社会调查	
	人员	素质	工作人员学历	拥有学士学位的工作人员数量占工作人员总数的比例
		结构	年龄结构	30—50岁工作人员占全体工作人员的比例
			性别结构	两性专业技术人员数量差与全体专业技术人员数量的比例
	价值观	导向管理	明确的价值观和使命感	
	技术	专业技术能力	专业技术人员学历	

续表

一级指标	二级指标	三级指标	四级指标	五级指标
影响力	政策影响力	对政策制定的影响力	政府委托研究项目	数量
			研究人员受邀为省部级及以上政府授课、接受省部级及以上政府咨询	人次
		与政府及决策者的关系	旋转门	曾经在省部级政府任职（包括挂职）的工作人员数量占工作人员总数的比例
				离开机构到省部级政府任职的工作人员数量占工作人员总数的比例
				在省部级政府兼职的工作人员数量占工作人员总数的比例
				曾任省部级及以上政府官员的工作人员数量占工作人员总数的比例
				离开机构任省部级及以上政府官员的工作人员数量占工作人员总数的比例
			官员培训	
	学术影响力	成果发布	出版连续出版物	数量
			发布研究报告、发表学术论文、出版学术著作	专业技术人员公开发布研究报告、发表学术论文的数量
				专业技术人员提交非公开研究报告的数量
				专业技术人员出版学术著作的数量
		学术活动活跃度	举办会议	单独或联合举办公开学术研讨会、圆桌会议、论坛的次数
			学术交流	与国内其他学术机构互访总次数

续表

一级指标	二级指标	三级指标	四级指标	五级指标
影响力	社会影响力	媒体曝光度	人员媒体曝光度	专业技术人员在国家级广播、电视、报纸和网络媒体发表政策性观点的总次数
			机构媒体曝光度	机构获得国家级广播、电视、报纸、网络媒体报道（含转载）的总次数
		社会责任	社会公益项目	开展社会公益项目的数量
		信息公开度	研究成果开放获取	
			网站内容	丰富性
			网站更新频率	
			成果推送	
	国际影响力	国际合作	与国外机构联合举办学术研讨会、圆桌会议、论坛的总次数	
			与国外机构或个人合作发布学术成果总件数	
			派往国外进行学术访问，参与学术交流、研讨会的总人次	
		注册国外分支机构	数量	
		外籍专业技术人员	外籍专业技术人员数量占专业技术人员总数的比例	
		使用多语种	专业技术人员公开发布研究报告、发表学术论文使用语言	总数
			机构网站语言版本	数量

（三）全球智库综合评价指标体系的特点

第一，评价指标注重定性与定量相结合。这是与以往智库评价方法的一个显著的不同之处。回顾已有的全球智库评价，我们深知必须突破单纯依靠主观定性评价方法的瓶颈，构建全面的定性加定量的评价指标体系。

第二，指标体系设计契合智库的工作流程。即从吸引力、管理力和影响力方面做了分析。吸引力好似一个漏斗，显示智库的外在声誉，对外界的吸引能力；管理力好似孵化器，展示智库的内在运作能力，即智库如何提高内部的有效管理，提高产出能力；影响力好似喇叭，展现智库的对外传播、政策作用等能力。这三种力相互作用，影响力大了则会反哺到吸引力，而吸引力加大则会促使更多的高品质人员聚集到智库，提升管理水平。

第三，指标覆盖面广。具体而言，吸引力包括声誉吸引力、人员吸引力、产品/成果吸引力和资金吸引力；管理力按照7S理论包括：战略（strategy）、组织（structure）、系统（system）、人员（staff）、风格（style）、价值观（shared value）和技术（skills）；影响力则包括政策影响力、学术影响力、社会影响力和国际影响力。

　　第四，充分发挥了专家群体和第三方评估的作用。此评价体系既发挥了专家评议的作用，又重视借鉴第三方评估的成果。前者专家评估的分值高达40分，后者第三方评估的分值为10分，两者合计占比超过了评价指标体系2015试用版中一级指标吸引力总分值82分的一半，这充分体现出评价指标体系对同行评议的高度重视。

四　全球智库评价过程与排行榜

（一）　全球智库评价过程

1. 调研过程

（1）　界定来源智库

课题组综合现有国内外智库评价成果，利用互联网、相关著作等对全球重要智库及基本信息进行了摸排和初步收集，并邀请各学科专家推荐本学科的重要智库。在对全球智库特征有了基本了解的基础上，对智库进行了界定，据此逐步缩小来源智库范围。

（2）　修订来源智库范围

专家咨询与实地调研贯串于项目进行的全过程。课题组多次邀请国内外智库，以及社会统计、信息管理、智库所涉及的各学科专家，就来源智库和评价体系进行研讨，并携带智库调查表和专家调查表走访了国内外多家智库，根据咨询与调研的反馈信息对来源智库进行了增删，最终确定来源智库1781家。

（3）　发放专家评分问卷及智库调查表

为了使主观评价主体的范围尽可能广泛，课题组进行了大量的专家搜集工作。根据智库的研究内容（地区＋专业领域），课题组将 1781 家智库划入 39 个大类，在每个大类中寻找为该类智库评分的专家。专家来源覆盖世界主要国家和地区的各专业及各行业，共发放专家问卷 20162 份。

同时，在客观评价数据方面，课题组通过邮件、电话、实地走访等方式尝试与所有来源智库建立直接联系，送达智库调查表 1575 份，回收有效调查表 156 份，43 家智库拒绝参与本次评价。课题组从 1781 家来源智库中挑选出 359 家最具影响力的智库，对其中没有返回调查表的智库进行人工信息搜集，以期做到重点智库不遗漏。

（4）数据统计

对于反馈和搜集的大量智库信息、专家评分及建议，课题组进行了认真、系统的记录和整理，对未反馈调查表的重要智库进行人工信息搜集，初步建立起全球重要智库数据库和智库专家数据库，并根据评价指标及权重对 359 家智库的数据进行了分数核算。

2. 调研方法

（1）一手资料的搜集

实地调研：课题组先后对美国、英国、德国、比利时、日本、韩国以及中国大陆及港台地区的百余家重点智库进行了实地调研，与智库负责人及研究人员进行了座谈，主要调研这些智库的运营模式、研究内容、观点输出渠道及影响决策的方式。

问卷调研：课题组通过向专家及智库发送和回收电子问卷与纸质问卷，获得专家评分及智库数据，作为主客观评价的基本依据。

电话调研：对于通过邮件未能取得联系的智库，课题组采用电话调研的方式，向智库介绍项目内容，解答智库的疑问，与相关负责人建立联系并发送问卷、获取智库的相关数据。

专家座谈：课题组十分重视各领域专家的意见。在整个调研过程中，除与实地走访的智库专家进行深入座谈外，课题组还利用国内外智库来访、举办及参加研讨会等机会，与各国各领域专家充分交换意见，听取其对本项目的意见和建议，并据此不断修正、完善本项目。

（2）二手资料的搜集

网络搜集：在调研过程中，课题组充分利用互联网资源，通过公开信息及数据库，搜集智库信息、专家信息、研究成果等，这些信息为项目的开展和完成提供了重要的基础。

图书资料：在本项目实施之前，世界上已有众多专家学者对智库进行了方方面面的研究，并撰写了一定数量的著作。项目组成员针对各自所负责的地区查阅了相关著作，以把握各地区的智库情况，有根据地确定该地区的来源智库。

研究报告：对已发布的中外智库评价报告，项目组进行了认真的研究，汲取其中成功的研究方法和评价体系，并努力改进其需要完善的方面。此外，在搜集智库信息及撰写国别智库报告时，项目组对所涉及的智库发布的研究报告进行了内容分析。

智库简介：根据智库官方网站所公布的信息，项目组为全球286家重点智库编译了中文版的智库简介，旨在为国内智库研究提供国内外更多智库的基本信息，以期进一步深入研究。

（二）全球智库排行榜

本排行榜所列的是 AMI 总分排在前 100 位的智库，共有 31 个国家/国际组织的智库上榜。其分布情况为：美国 18 家，德国 11 家，中国、日本各 9 家，韩国 6 家，比利时 5 家，意大利、英国各 4 家，巴西、智利各 3 家，国际组织、阿根廷、荷兰、加拿大、南非、瑞士、印度各 2 家，波兰、法国、芬兰、吉尔吉斯斯坦、挪威、瑞典、土耳其、西班牙、希腊、新加坡、以色列、阿塞拜疆、埃及、澳大利亚各 1 家。

需要说明的是，课题组所在的中国社会科学评价中心隶属于中国社会科学院，为保证评价的客观公正，未将中国社会科学院及其所属智库纳入本排行榜。

表 7　　　　　　　　　　全球智库排行榜

排名	国家/国际组织	机构名称	AMI	A	M	I
1	美国	卡内基国际和平基金会	179.56	64.56	53.00	62.00
2	比利时	布鲁盖尔	178.20	63.20	54.00	61.00
3	美国	传统基金会	175.00	60.00	51.00	64.00
4	英国	查塔姆社——皇家国际事务研究所	172.00	64.00	41.00	67.00
5	瑞典	斯德哥尔摩国际和平研究所	170.00	62.00	51.00	57.00
6	美国	布鲁金斯学会	169.40	73.40	48.00	48.00
7	德国	康拉德·阿登纳基金会	169.00	58.00	43.00	68.00
8	美国	伍德罗·威尔逊国际学者中心	168.36	64.36	45.00	59.00
9	中国	国务院发展研究中心	168.32	51.32	48.00	69.00
10	英国	国际战略研究所	160.00	57.00	45.00	58.00
11	日本	公益财团法人日本国际问题研究所	157.60	68.60	30.00	59.00
12	日本	防卫研究所	154.82	66.32	30.00	58.50

排名	国家/国际组织	机构名称	AMI	A	M	I
13	美国	外交关系委员会	153.64	67.64	34.00	52.00
14	英国	海外发展研究所	152.36	57.36	40.00	55.00
15	日本	独立行政法人日本贸易振兴机构亚洲经济研究所	151.56	56.56	35.00	60.00
16	韩国	科学技术政策研究院	151.36	51.36	29.00	71.00
17	英国	欧洲改革中心	150.64	51.64	46.00	53.00
18	德国	生态研究所	150.36	54.36	34.00	62.00
19	美国	战略与国际研究中心	150.04	61.04	41.00	48.00
20	德国	贝塔斯曼基金会	150.00	48.00	34.00	68.00
21	韩国	韩国环境政策研究院	149.50	49.00	38.00	62.50
22	日本	东北大学东北亚研究中心	149.32	45.32	42.00	62.00
23	中国	中国国际问题研究院	147.80	54.80	36.00	57.00
24	瑞士	日内瓦安全政策中心	147.36	44.36	30.00	73.00
25	德国	德国发展研究所	146.40	61.40	42.00	43.00
26	意大利	意大利国际政治学研究院	145.36	54.36	33.00	58.00
27	美国	东西中心	145.18	59.68	46.00	39.50
28	国际组织	亚洲开发银行研究所	144.80	64.80	30.00	50.00
29	意大利	国际事务研究院	144.36	67.36	41.00	36.00
30	韩国	国立外交院外交事务和国家安全研究所	143.68	46.68	31.00	66.00
31	巴西	热图利奥·瓦加斯基金会	143.22	49.72	50.00	43.50
32	德国	慕尼黑大学莱布尼茨伊福经济研究所	142.40	56.40	45.00	41.00
33	日本	公益财团法人地球环境战略研究机构	142.20	54.20	47.00	41.00

续表

排名	国家/国际组织	机构名称	AMI	A	M	I
34	西班牙	皇家埃尔卡诺研究院	142.00	55.00	32.00	55.00
35	中国	中国现代国际关系研究院	141.70	57.20	38.00	46.50
36	比利时	国际危机小组	141.64	62.64	41.00	38.00
36	日本	公益财团法人东京财团	141.64	58.64	28.00	55.00
38	美国	彼得森国际经济研究所	141.00	47.00	36.00	58.00
39	日本	独立行政法人经济产业研究所	140.20	53.20	42.00	45.00
40	法国	政治创新基金会	139.66	54.16	43.00	42.50
40	中国	中国国际经济交流中心	139.66	51.16	38.00	50.50
42	加拿大	费雷泽研究所	139.16	54.16	44.00	41.00
43	希腊	希腊欧洲与外交政策基金会	139.00	62.00	43.00	34.00
44	日本	株式会社三菱综合研究所	138.90	49.40	28.00	61.50
45	比利时	欧洲国际政治经济研究中心	138.64	51.64	41.00	46.00
46	美国	新美国安全中心	137.00	55.00	37.00	45.00
47	瑞士	瑞士和平基金会	136.60	56.60	45.00	35.00
48	阿根廷	阿根廷国际关系委员会	136.00	51.00	35.00	50.00
48	美国	未来资源	136.00	56.00	36.00	44.00
50	挪威	奥斯陆和平研究院	135.36	65.36	23.00	47.00
51	比利时	欧洲政策中心	135.00	60.00	33.00	42.00
51	美国	世界资源研究所	135.00	59.00	42.00	34.00
53	德国	科学与政治基金会——德国国际政治与安全研究所	134.86	50.36	30.00	54.50
54	日本	国立研究开发法人产业技术综合研究所	134.80	57.80	30.00	47.00
55	德国	基尔大学世界经济研究所	134.36	54.36	45.00	35.00
56	智利	公共研究中心	134.04	46.04	46.00	42.00
57	阿塞拜疆	经济与社会发展中心	134.00	48.00	29.00	57.00
57	以色列	国家安全研究所	134.00	57.00	38.00	39.00

续表

排名	国家/国际组织	机构名称	AMI	A	M	I
59	印度	德里政策集团	133.64	45.64	36.00	52.00
59	印度	能源与资源研究所	133.64	55.64	38.00	40.00
59	中国	国家发展和改革委员会宏观经济研究院	133.64	44.64	41.00	48.00
62	美国	预算和政策优先研究中心	133.00	61.00	38.00	34.00
62	美国	斯坦福大学胡佛研究所	133.00	56.00	36.00	41.00
62	南非	非洲建设性解决争端研究中心	133.00	58.00	38.00	37.00
65	土耳其	萨班大学伊斯坦布尔政策中心	132.64	46.64	22.00	64.00
66	智利	拉美研究公司	132.04	43.04	50.00	39.00
67	波兰	社会与经济研究中心	132.00	62.00	35.00	35.00
67	美国	美国和平研究所	132.00	57.00	42.00	33.00
67	南非	南非国际事务研究所	132.00	56.00	41.00	35.00
67	中国	商务部国际贸易经济合作研究院	132.00	41.00	50.00	41.00
71	吉尔吉斯斯坦	中亚自由市场研究所	131.98	40.48	30.00	61.50
72	美国	美洲国家对话	131.64	56.64	36.00	39.00
73	荷兰	荷兰克林根达尔国际关系研究院	131.00	56.00	38.00	37.00
73	意大利	埃尼·恩里科·马特艾基金会	131.00	65.00	27.00	39.00
75	比利时	艾格蒙皇家国际关系研究所	130.40	58.40	27.00	45.00
76	阿根廷	公平与增长公共政策实施中心	130.32	43.32	45.00	42.00
77	德国	德国外交政策学会	130.20	52.20	42.00	36.00
78	韩国	韩国开发研究院	129.64	47.64	43.00	39.00
79	巴西	费尔南多·恩里克·卡多佐研究所	129.50	44.00	45.00	40.50
80	澳大利亚	洛伊国际政策研究所	129.40	51.40	21.00	57.00
81	新加坡	东南亚研究所	129.36	47.36	35.00	47.00
82	芬兰	芬兰国际事务研究院	129.20	57.20	36.00	36.00

续表

排名	国家/国际组织	机构名称	AMI	A	M	I
83	意大利	欧洲—地中海气候变化研究中心	129.00	54.00	42.00	33.00
84	中国	清华大学国情研究院	128.80	51.80	32.00	45.00
85	加拿大	麦克唐纳·劳里埃研究所	128.64	52.64	34.00	42.00
86	美国	城市研究所	128.04	61.04	37.00	30.00
87	德国	黑森和平与冲突研究基金会	128.00	48.00	43.00	37.00
87	德国	波茨坦气候影响研究所	128.00	68.00	27.00	33.00
87	中国	中国人民大学国家发展与战略研究院	128.00	56.00	35.00	37.00
90	美国	世界政治研究所	127.64	47.64	44.00	36.00
91	韩国	峨山政策研究院	127.04	48.04	31.00	48.00
92	荷兰	欧洲发展政策管理中心	127.00	59.00	37.00	31.00
93	埃及	经济研究论坛	126.36	52.36	38.00	36.00
94	智利	自由与发展	126.20	45.20	41.00	40.00
95	巴西	巴西国际关系中心	126.16	46.16	40.00	40.00
96	中国	北京大学国家发展研究院	125.80	42.80	35.00	48.00
97	国际组织	世界银行研究所	125.54	53.04	33.00	39.50
98	德国	弗里德里希·瑙曼自由基金会	125.50	53.00	38.00	34.50
99	韩国	韩国教育课程评价院	125.00	42.00	35.00	48.00
100	美国	兰德公司	124.40	58.40	38.00	28.00

五 基于全球视角审视中国特色新型智库的构建

（一） 智库罗盘

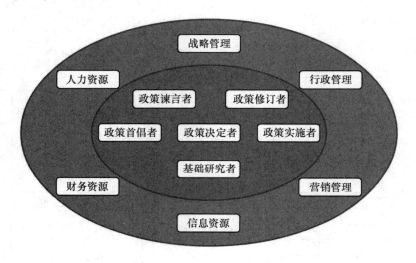

图3 智库罗盘

资料来源：课题组制作。

我们认为，智库罗盘是构建智库的核心路径，既要致力于智库的基础层的建设，具体包括：战略管理、行政管理、营销管理，整合信息资源、财务资源、人力资源等，形成坚实的智库基础层；与此同时，为了提升智库的竞争力，智库必须对政策制定的相关人员进行影响，包括基础研究者、政策首倡者、政策谏言者、政策决定者、政策修订者和政策实施者。

（二）关于"中国特色新型智库热"的冷思考

中共中央办公厅、国务院办公厅印发《关于加强中国特色新型智库建设的意见》（以下简称《意见》）之后，我国掀起了"智库热"。然而，要建设具有国际影响力、世界知名的中国特色新型智库，必须冷静思考。

我国的"智库热"体现在如下几个方面：

第一，热在数量——重视智库数量的增加，而忽略了智库质量的提高。党的十八大以来，习近平总书记从推动科学决策、民主决策，推进国家治理体系和治理能力现代化和增强国家软实力的战略高度，就加强中国特色新型智库建设多次作出重要论述。特别是，2015 年 1 月的《意见》把中国的智库热推到高潮。有的专家认为，仅最近两年以来，我国新挂牌的各类智库就远远不止 1 万家。[①] 对此，我们估算新建的智库有5000 家左右。这种高速发展的确是惊人的，单纯从数

---

① 陈永杰：《建设中国特色新型智库要纠正异化、制止乱象》，《经济观察报》2015 年 5 月 25 日。

量上看，我国的智库数量早已位居世界第一。但是，这显然有违中央号召加强智库建设的初衷——2013年4月，习近平总书记就加强中国特色新型智库建设作出明确批示："智库是国家软实力的重要组成部分，随着形势的发展，智库的作用会越来越大，要高度重视、积极探索中国特色新型智库的组织形式和管理形式。"2013年11月在中国共产党十八届三中全会上通过的《中共中央关于全面深化改革若干重大问题的决定》再次强调："加强中国特色新型智库建设，建立健全决策咨询制度。"究其本意，智库的质量是本，建立健全的决策咨询制度，才是加强中国特色新型智库建设的原动力。

第二，热在排行榜——重视智库的排行，而忽略了智库的整体建设。在美国宾夕法尼亚大学发布《全球智库报告》之初，该报告在国内外的影响并不大，而且其使用的智库评价体系等尚存在诸多问题。但是，随着中国"智库热"的出现，许多智库把精力放在了智库排行上，该榜单也随之成为各方面的关注焦点，而该项目的负责人麦甘也成为国内众多智库论坛上的嘉宾。与此同时，由上海社会科学院、零点国际发展研究院与中国网分别发布的"中国智库报告"都针对国内智库的影响力做出了评价，进而把各方智库的关注点再次吸引到排名位次上，而忽略了智库的整体建设。

第三，热在传播——重视智库的宣传工作，而忽略了智库的核心工作是公共政策研究。不可否认，过去我国的智库不太重视智库成果的对外宣传，将许多研究成果束之高阁，没有对相关的决策部门、意见领袖和社会大众进行充分的反馈。所以，智库的一项重要工作是对国内外的宣传。但是，绝不能矫枉过正——把宣传工作作为智库的首要任务，而忽略了智库的核心工作是对公共政策的研究。我们发现，近来个别的国内智库热衷于上媒体、办论坛，甚至哗众取宠，造势作秀，而没有把主要的精力放在资政研究上。这种本末倒置的做法，不仅仅没有引起大家的警觉，反而当事人乐在其中，并且带来大量的模仿者。如果此风潮继续下去，长此以往，后果不堪设想。

第四，热在跟风——重视热点问题的跟踪研究，而忽略了开拓性的创新型研究。智库贵在有自己的侧重方向，有自己的研究特色，乃至有自己对相关问题的独立见解。而今我国的许多智库热衷于对时下热点问题的跟踪，这样，难免出现"千库一面""万库一声"的尴尬局面。建设中国特色新型智库的难点在于如何让中国智库掌控议题的设置权，掌握话语权，这就势必要避免千篇一律、人云亦云的模仿型研究，需要开拓新的研究领域，从国家利益的高度出发，以我为主、替我所言、为我所用，真正发挥智库资政议政的作用。

综上所述，"智库热"在中国有其客观的必然需求，也有人为因素。在这股热潮中，我们不应失去理性，应当高度关注"智库热"的特征，防止燥热带来的盲目与冲动，破坏了智库发展的大好环境。同时，要对智库建设加以引导，求真务实，稳扎稳打；以质为本，做好基础建设工作；树立问题导向，加强政策研究；资政与宣传并重，内部修炼与外部推广兼有；掌握议题，创新资政，兼收并蓄，开放协同。只有如此，中国特色新型智库的春天才会持续长久。

（三）建设中国特色新型智库提升文化软实力

建设具有中国特色的新型智库，是提升我国文化软实力的实际需要。

"软实力"（soft power）一词最早是由美国哈佛大学

教授约瑟夫·奈在 1990 年提出来的。当时，他分别在
《外交政策》和《政治学季刊》杂志上发表了《软实力》
和《变化中的世界力量的本质》等一系列论文，[①]并在
此基础上出版了《美国定能领导世界吗》一书。[②]约瑟
夫·奈认为：一个国家的综合国力既包括由经济、科技、
军事实力等表现出来的"硬实力"，也包括以文化和意
识形态吸引力体现出来的"软实力"。文化软实力是国
家软实力的核心因素，是指一个国家或地区文化的影响
力、凝聚力和感召力。

改革开放三十多年来，我国的硬实力得到极大的提
升。首先，从经济实力来看：1980 年我国的国民生产总
值在全球位列第七名，虽然在 1990 年曾一度下滑到第十
名，但是到 2000 年就已超过了意大利、加拿大、西班牙
和巴西，位居第六名；2005 年超过法国，位居第五名；
2006 年超过英国，位居第四名；2007 年超过德国，位居
第三名。到 2010 年第二季度，我国的国民生产总值就已

---

① Joseph S. Nye, Jr., "Soft Power", *Foreign Policy*, No. 80, Twentieth Anniversary (Autumn 1990); Joseph S. Nye, Jr., "The Changing Nature of World Power", *Political Science Quarterly*, Vol. 105, No. 2 (Summer 1990).

② ［美］约瑟夫·奈：《美国定能领导世界吗》，何小东等译，军事译文出版社 1992 年版。

经超过了日本，位居世界第二名。[①]

再从科技实力来看。国家统计局发布的《新中国 60 周年系列报告之十六》指出，新中国成立 60 年来，我国科技实力明显增强，科技创新硕果累累，社会资源配置对自主研发的倾斜逐年加大。我国研发投入总量紧随美国、日本、德国、法国、英国之后，位居世界第六。2008 年我国全社会研究与试验发展经费支出与国内生产总值（GDP）之比为 1.52%，比 1991 年增加了 0.87 个百分点。[②] 到 2012 年我国研究与试验发展（R&D）经费总量突破万亿元大关之后，经费投入强度（经费投入与国内生产总值之比）在 2013 年首次突破 2%，达到 2.08%，比上一年的 1.98% 提高了 0.1 个百分点。这些都充分表明我国科技实力不断增强，与美、日等发达国家的差距进一步缩小。[③]

---

① 荆林波等：《中国中长期贸易战略》，中国社会科学出版社 2015 年版，第 76 页。

② 国家统计局：《我国研发经费与 GDP 之比达到 1.52%》，新华社网址，2009 年 9 月 25 日。

③ 国家统计局、科学技术部、财政部联合发布的《2013 年全国科技经费投入公报》显示，2013 年，全国共投入研究与试验发展（R&D）经费 11846.6 亿元，比上年增加 1548.2 亿元，增长 15%；按研究与试验发展人员（全时工作量）计算的人均经费为 33.5 万元，比上年增加 1.8 万元。

最后从军事实力来看，中国的国防预算一直在逐步增长，2014 年增长了 12.2%，为 1260 亿美元。但就军人人均经费而言，中国的国防预算人均仅为几万美元，中国军队规模庞大，现役部队人数为 228 万人，预备部队为 230 万人。无论是媒体的排名或是军事专家的分析，即便是美国《国防防务周刊》的排名，我国的军事实力普遍位列全球第三名。美国《商业内幕》网站推出世界 35 强军队排行榜时，使用了现有各国军力数据库，主要以目前著名的"全球火力指数"（GFP）[①] 排行榜为基础。GFP 排行榜是世界最权威的军事排行榜之一，其数据库主要收集世界各国的军队信息，并进行分析和总结。根据《商业内幕》的数据，排名世界前十的军事大国依次为美国、俄罗斯、中国、印度、英国、法国、德国、土耳其、韩国和日本。

---

① "全球火力指数"使用了复杂的评估方法，考虑 50 多个不同因素，根据相关计算结果，得到一个大致反映某国军队实力的评分（火力指数）。同时，为了保证评估尽可能地客观，使用加分和扣分系统，另外增加几项附加条件，主要包括：评估时不考虑核武器；评估时考虑国家地理特点；评估对象不只是武器装备数量；评估时考虑某些资源的生产和消费；没有出海口的国家不会因为缺少海军而扣分；海军能力有限将会扣分；评估时不考虑国家政治和军事领导人的特点。引自《2014 年全球（世界）军力排行榜出炉——中国军力排名第三》，铁血网 2014 年 8 月 16 日（http://bbs. tiexue. net/post2_ 8265750_ 1. html）。

然而，在我国硬实力提升的同时，我国的软实力却没有得到长足的进步，仍然存在着诸多短板。

第一，在核心价值体系方面，我国仍然处于西方话语体系的边缘，话语体系构建相对滞后于内涵丰富的中国道路实践，[①] 以讲"中国故事"、客观解读"中国奇迹"、共同铸就"中国梦"的价值理念与理论体系有待进一步完善。

第二，在文化产品和文化服务方面，无论是对传统文化元素的挖掘与利用，还是利用现代技术开发新的文化产品和服务，我国都存在着较大的潜力。如何传承和发扬光大五千年的中华文明、如何在新的信息文明中不错失发展机会，都需要统筹规划、协同攻关。

第三，在微观基础方面，我国公民的整体素质有待提高，社会公德、职业道德、家庭美德和个人品德等都有待提升，使国民具备与大国风范相匹配的文明修养，实现名副其实的"礼仪之邦"需要继续努力。

第四，在国际传播体系方面，以美国为代表的西方传播力量依然强势，我国总体上处于被动应付的状态，

---

① 李韬、林经纬：《中国软实力提升：问题与出路》，《红旗文稿》2013 年 7 月 9 日。

尤其是众多版本的"中国威胁论"给中国软实力带来了巨大的负面影响。因此，如何将被动应对转变为主动出击，如何破除"中国威胁论"的魔咒都还需要持之以恒的努力。

习近平总书记在主持中央政治局 2013 年第十二次集体学习时便已指出，提高国家文化软实力，关系到"两个一百年"奋斗目标和中华民族伟大复兴中国梦的实现。① 而所有这些内容，与构建中国特色新型智库紧密相关，智库是国家软实力的重要载体，越来越成为国际竞争力的重要因素。诚如习近平总书记所作的阐述：围绕努力夯实国家文化软实力的根基、努力传播当代中国价值观念、努力展示中华文化独特魅力、努力提高国际话语权四个方面，是建设社会主义文化强国、提高国家文化软实力的根本指引，同样也是构建中国特色新型智库的实际需要。

（四）建设中国特色新型智库推进国家治理现代化

《中共中央关于全面深化改革若干重大问题的决定》

---

① 慎海雄：《让我们的文化软实力硬起来》，《瞭望》2014 年第 2 期。

指出，"全面深化改革的总目标是完善和发展中国特色社会主义制度，推进国家治理体系和治理能力现代化"。我们认为，这充分体现了与时俱进的治理理念，切中了我国国家运行中的核心问题。而所有这些都与建设中国特色新型智库紧密相关。

第一，顺应了全球治理的要求，智库必须有全球视野。1990 年，社会党国际前主席、国际发展委员会主席、联邦德国前总理勃兰特首次提出"全球治理"的概念。1991 年，在瑞典的会议上，参会人员发表了《关于全球安全与管理的斯德哥尔摩倡议》，提出建立与发展多边规则和管理体系以促进全球相互依存与可持续发展。1992 年，28 位国际知名人士发起成立了"全球治理委员会"（Commission on Global Governance）。1995 年，在联合国成立五十周年之际，全球治理委员会发表了《天涯成比邻》（*Our Global Neighborhood*）的研究报告，第一次较为系统地阐述了全球治理的概念、价值以及全球治理同经济全球化、全球安全的关系。根据全球治理委员会的定义：治理是个人和制度、公共和私营部门管理其共同事务的各种方法的综合。它是一个持续的过程，其中，冲突或多元利益能够相互协调并能采取合作行动，它既包括正式的制度安排，也包括非正式的制度安排。所谓全球治理，指的是通过具有约束力的国际规制和有效的国际合作，解决全球性的政治、经济、生态和安全问题（包括全球性的冲突、人权、移民、毒品、走私、传染病等问题），以维持正常的国际政治经济秩序。为了顺应全球治理的浪潮，我国应当构建自己的全球治理理论。深化对全球化和全球治理的研究，正确认识全球治理的实质和规律，根据我国的特点和国家利益，形成中国自己的全球化理论和全球治理观。当然，构建我国自己的全球治理理论，当务之急是构建我国的国家治理理论，夯实基础。而这就需要我国的智库积极参与其中，建言献策，分享治理智慧。

当今世界，全球治理的话题已经超越传统的政治、经济话题，日益扩大到诸如气候变化、网络安全等领域，这些话题的专业化程度越来越高，迫切需要专业化的智库提供相应的解决方案。再比如，在全球共治与分治的矛盾中，中国作为一个新兴的大国，如何与发达国家（特别是美国）处理好关系，如何理顺我国与金砖国家之间的关系，如何处理我国与周边国家的关系，这些都需要相关智库开展有针对性的研究，筹划出长期的、战略性的建议。

第二，顺应了我国国家综合国力提高的要求，我国智库必须有全方位解决问题的能力。综合国力的竞争，是全球化时代国家间竞争的根本所在。促进经济的发展，增加国家的经济总量，提高人民的生活水平，巩固国防力量，是提高综合国力的基本途径。但是，在全球化时代，综合国力的其他要素也变得日益重要，例如，国民的文化、教育、心理和身体素质，国家的科学技术水平，民族文化的优越性和先进性，国家的人才资源和战略人才储备情况，政府的合法性与凝聚力，社会的团结和稳定程度，经济和社会发展的可持续性，等等。我们应当清楚地认识到，在参与全球治理的过程中，要有效地维护国家的主权，仅有经济的和军事的力量是远远不够的，还必须有政治的、文化的和道义的力量。全面推进社会主义经济建设、政治建设、文化建设、社会建设、生态文明建设，加快发展社会主义市场经济、民主政治、先进文化、和谐社会、生态文明，这都需要从国家治理体系的建设入手，都需要各类智库提出合理化建议。

第三，顺应了我国全面深化改革的要求，智库必须要努力破解时代难题。"经济体制改革是全面深化改革的重点，核心问题是处理好政府和市场的关系，使市场在资源配置中起决定性作用和更好发挥政府作用。"国家治理水平的高低体现在如何协调各种利益群体，充分发挥市场与政府的不同作用。比如，回顾我国的房地产调控政策，其调控的基调是以住房需求管理为主、以调控供应为辅，把"支持自住需求、抑制投机投资性购房"作为房地产市场调控必须坚持的一项基本政策。特别是，从2010年开始，更为严厉的调控政策相继出台。这些政策固然很好，可是在执行中面临着房屋产权确认难、第二套房屋认定标准统一难和异地购房标准掌握难等众多困难；更为极端的是，有些人利用假离婚来规避第二套房屋产权的认定，使得相关调控政策落空。限贷、限购、限价以及各地出台的限制外地人购房四管齐下，加上房产税试点、二手房征20%个人所得税等手段，如此严厉的需求调控措施，仍无法收到预期的效果，这的确值得我们反思。也从一个侧面说明，我国的智库在此类问题上谏言不足或者无法击中要害。调控措施过多地集中于住房需求上，实际上是抑制需求，而且这些调控政策没有很好地对住房的需求进行细分，也没有采取区别对待的措施。仅仅简单靠调控政策无法理顺多元化需求，无法从根本上区分哪些是民众的基本住房需求、哪些是投机性需求。以往的以调控需求为主的政策无非是增加了购房者的交易成本，对于投机者而言，他们会把这些成本进一步转嫁出去，而对于那些自住的基本需求者而言，尤其是低收入阶层而言，则有苦难言。即使从住房需求调控入手，也要避免眉毛胡子一把抓，绝不能混淆政府补贴与市场调剂的对象，必须充分发挥政府保障与市场调节的功能。

除此之外，金融政策、财税政策乃至"一带一路"等国家大政方针，都需要智库在其中发挥引领作用，而且随着改革的深化，政府越来越倚重于智库的参谋作用，我们坚信智库的作用会越来越重要。

第四，顺应了建立整体的国家安全战略的需要，我国智库必须担负国家使命。任何国家都应当对全球安全负起自己的责任，但大国的责任更多。中国不仅在维和、军控、防止核扩散等方面负有重要责任，而且在全球经济安全、生态安全和地区安全方面的责任也更加重大。同时，全球化时代也是信息时代和网络时代，国家安全的内容和形式都发生了重大的变化，信息安全的重要变得前所未有。因此，我们的智库也必须顺应国家安全战略需要，应当有一种新的整体国家安全观。目前，我国已经设立国家安全委员会，完善国家安全体制和国家安全战略，确保国家安全。除了维护领土完整、民族尊严和国防安全以外，也应把降低金融风险和对外经济依赖、保障战略资源储备、保护战略人才、弘扬民族文化、维护生态平衡、保证物种安全、反对国际恐怖主义等，提高到维护国家主权和国家自主的高度，这都需要智库与时俱进，考虑从政治、经济、军事、科技、文化、教育、信息、资源、人才、生态等多个方面，为国家献计献策，增强国家抵御全球风险的能力，保证我国在积极参与全球治理过程中的独立自主。

（五）破解构建中国特色新型智库的三大难题

第一，独立性的问题。众所周知，目前全球智库发展最为发达的美国，其构建智库的一个基本理念是独立性。而如今，我们创建中国特色的新型智库，也面临着如何彰显智库的独立性的问题。

独立性体现在一方面是财务的独立性，另一方面是观点立场的独立性。就财务的独立性而言，目前我国的大多数智库是由政府出资建立，故而很难在短期内转变为依靠社会筹资运营的智库机构。对此，我们可以通过鼓励民间资本投入新兴智库建设中，也可以鼓励社会资本设立相关议题的方式，来逐步扩大资本的多元化。就观点立场的独立性而言，这是国外一些机构与人员对我国智库批评较多的地方，他们认为中国的智库存在着依附政府的倾向，只能做政策的解读，而无法独立发声，难以发挥智库应有的咨政议政的作用。拿了政府的钱、隶属于政府，是否就意味着不能独立发声？在这个问题上，需要我们大胆创新，开拓新的渠道，谋求新的路径。我们认为，在不违背大政方针的前提下，对具体的公共政策，应该鼓励相关智库提出各自的独立观点，以免政府决策部门在单一思维惯性下作出错误的决策。所以，开放、包容、理性与分享的社会环境，不仅是当下我国智库建设的必要条件，也是推进我国智库独立性建设的一个重要环节。

第二，多元化的问题。独立性与多元化紧密相关。首先，多元化体现在智库类型的多元化，不仅要有政府背景的智库，还要有民间的智库；不仅要有来自科研机构、高校的智库，也要有来自政府支撑机构、专业团体、新闻媒体构建的智库；不仅要有国内的智库，而且也要有外国的智库。其次，多元化体现在有不同的声音、不同的解决方案，提供决策者作为参考备选。不同的智库发表自己的不同主张和看法，也体现了社会的理性宽容和多元化进步。最后，多元化体现在智库的特色上。一枝独秀不是春，百花齐放春满园。这要求我们的中国特色新型智库必须在"特"字上下功夫，专注相关领域的问题，培养专业的队伍，形成各自的特长。美国的智库在这方面做出了表率：比如，美国的兰德公司见长于军事研究，进而不断扩大到国际问题研究；美国的战略与国际研究中心以研究外交政策为主，与英国的国际战略研究所并称为世界上顶级的研究国际战略的智库；而美国企业研究所是美国保守派的重要政策研究机构，与共和党渊源较深，许多共和党重要官员纷纷加入该所，故舆论界又称它为共和党的"影子内阁""流亡政府"，与布鲁金斯学会并称为美国华盛顿的"两大思想库"，也有人称它为"保守的布鲁金斯"。

第三，话语权的问题。不仅仅是国内话语权的主导问题，更重要的是国际话语权的主导问题。纵观智库的发展历程，我们可以清楚地发现，智库的一个核心作用在于掌握话语权，创设新的议题，引导国内外舆论的走向。比如，成立于 1977 年的卡托研究所，深受亚当·斯密的古典自由主义思想的影响，主张减少政府对于国内政治、经济和社会的干预，并且减少在国际上的政治和军事干预。为此，它总是能够提出一系列的相关议题与政策建议，具体包括：在经济上，减少联邦政府对市场运作以及地方州政府的干预、废止最低工资管制、废止企业补助和贸易壁垒；在社会相关政策上，深化自由学校选择制度、废止政府实行的族群歧视政策、改革反毒品政策，等等。再比如，所谓"中美共治"（G2）、"中美欧大三角"（G3）等热议话题背后都是智库专家们的精心策划。

当然，我们欣喜地看到我们在"一带一路"、亚洲基础设施投资银行等话题方面已经取得了初步的成果，但是，我们希望中国特色新型智库在越来越多的国内外舞台上发出更多的声音，引领国际的话语走向。

（六）建设中国特色新型智库必须处理好六大关系

第一，处理好基础研究与对策研究的关系。科研机构与大学关注基础研究，是要解决"是什么"和"为什么"的问题，将复杂现实简化，抽出关键变量，找出它们之间的逻辑关系，并进行合理阐释。而思想库和智囊团——智库关注的更多是对策研究。对策研究则是解决"怎么办"的问题，需要超越基础研究，既涉及对政策的理解和把握，又需要丰富的实践经验和强烈的问题意识，并且重在寻求现实问题的解决之道。基础研究和对策研究之间是一种辩证发展关系，有了良好的基础研究做支撑，对策研究才能有力度与深度，否则对策研究将成为无源之水。因此，中国特色新型智库建设要理性，不能混淆基础研究和对策研究的关系。建设中国特色新型智库必须坚持基础研究与对策研究并举的方针，推出有客观依据、经得起实践和历史检验的原创性基础研究成果，使对策研究建立在深入扎实的基础研究之上。我们应当坚决反对一些所谓"智库"的做法——急功近利，为了获得"智库"的称号，短平快地推出系列"点子"，获得短期的关注度。

基础研究与对策研究，两者的侧重点不同，因此，在人、财、物有限的状况下，必须处理好两者的关系。鱼和熊掌不可兼得的情况下，如何做出取舍？尤其是，对于研究人员而言，要在基础研究与对策研究上都有所建树，实属不易。

第二，处理好科研考核与智库考核的关系。与第一点所对应，基础研究关注的是发表学术论文、出版专著等，而对策研究关注的是获得领导批示、有关部门的采纳，两者的考核体系不尽相同，如何在同一个机构内，平衡好对两类研究的考核，成为智库建设的一个核心问题。只有运用好考核这个指挥棒，才能充分调动各方面的积极性，参与到世界知名智库的建设中来。

第三，处理好练好内功与对外宣传的关系。练好内功是智库构建核心竞争力之所在。围绕马克思主义基本理论和中国特色社会主义理论体系，围绕经济社会发展重大问题和国际问题，开展全局性、战略性、前瞻性、系统性、综合性研究，推出现实性强、公信度高、影响力大的创新性理论观点和决策研究成果，为中央决策提供高质量的智力服务。要完成如此重任，练好内功是必不可少的。

同时，"酒香也怕巷子深"，智库的对外宣传也是至关重要的。纵览美国的著名智库，在对外宣传方面可谓不遗余力。比如，布鲁金斯学会、卡内基国际和平基金会，都设立了专门的机构与人员，负责成果的对外推广，并且建立了国内外的网络系统，立体化、多渠道地宣传自己的成果，特别是在互联网时代，加强了对网络媒体的运用，取得了较好的效果。这些成功经验值得我国的智库学习与借鉴。

第四，处理好智库建设与后勤保障的关系。智库的建设绝对离不开后勤保障体系的建设。我们认为，智库的后勤保障体系，至少应包括：数据支撑体系、日常行政运行体系、财务运营体系，等等。

首先，数据支撑体系是智库运行的基本保障。应对大数据时代的来临，我国的智库必须思考如何按照"云"构架，建立统一的、海量的哲学社会科学大型信息数据库；如何利用海量数据库构建起数据过滤系统，从而把握核心数据，建立起有效的决策支持系统；如何适应数字化的时代要求，建立快速反应的网络舆情反馈系统，帮助政府有关部门做好危机公关。

其次，日常行政运行体系是智库高效运行的保障。一直以来，日常行政运行效率低下的问题严重地影响了我国智库整体的效率。对此，国外智库的运行经验可以考虑借鉴一二。从现状来看，我们的研究人员要花费相当的精力去应付各种表格的填写、相关票据的处理，如此折腾过后真正用来做研究的时间受到了影响。其实，美国、英国的智库经验告诉我们，一名研究人员加一名研究助理的效率远远大于两名研究人员的效率之和。研究助理承担后勤保障，可以为研究人员节约大量的时间与精力，从而提高整个智库的效率。

最后，财务运营体系是智库运行的生命线。目前，政府全资拨款的智库尚不存在财务方面的压力，但独立运行的民间智库则必然会面对较大的财务压力。随着智库之间的竞争日益加剧，智库的运行能否有序、稳健，也与融资能力紧密相关。在欧美发达国家，智库领导人的重要职责之一就是募集资金，以保障智库的可持续发展。

第五，处理好立足中国与国际化的关系。中国特色新型智库显然要以解决中国实际问题为导向，以影响中国公共政策为对象，以追求中国国家利益最大化为目标，逐步打造具有中国话语体系的研究氛围。这里我们必须明确，中国特色新型智库绝不可能简单照搬国外已有智库的模式，尤其要防范"智库的美国化"倾向，防范智库议题被他人所掌控，防范出谋划策中出现卖国行为，损害国家的利益。

与此同时，坚持对外开放、兼收并蓄，加强与国际一流智库的交流，拓展交流的领域，深化交流的程度，尤其是要重视中国智库走出去，积极参与国际话题的讨论，发出自己的声音，并且要逐步引领一些话题的讨论方向，甚至要创造出一些议题，掌握国际的话语权。

第六，处理好专业人才与复合型人才的关系。智库的建设归根结底是人才队伍的建设，特别是如何构建一支高素质、跨学科、多类型的智库人才队伍。高素质要求智库人员具备国际视野，学贯中西，了解国情，熟悉国内政策环境；跨学科要求智库人员的知识结构要合理，一专多能，具备复合型知识结构；多类型要求智库人员具备跨领域工作的阅历，能够较好地与政府有关部门进行沟通，从而更好地发挥智库的影响作用。美国智库的一个特点在于存在"旋转门"机制，四年一次的大选，如果出现政党更替执政，那么，将有4000名左右的人员需要换岗，有相当一部分人员在政府与智库之间进行角色转换，这对政府和智库都有积极的作用。相对而言，我国目前智库与政府机构之间的人员流动比较少，这就要求智库人员更要积极地了解政府有关部门的运作程序、机制，从而更大程度地发挥咨政议政的功能。

全球智库评价项目大事记

2014 年 2 月 13 日，中国社会科学评价中心全球核心智库评价项目部成立。

2014 年 3 月 21 日，与中国社会科学院社会学研究所李炜研究员座谈，探讨智库评价的思路和方法。

2014 年 4 月 21 日，与中国人民大学统计学院院长赵彦云教授座谈，探讨智库评价中的统计问题。

2014 年 4 月 25 日，与院图书馆数据库网络部负责人杨齐等进行座谈，了解院图书馆数据库情况，讨论建设智库评价数据库问题。

2014 年 6 月 10—17 日，赴德国考察智库，访问波恩应用政治研究院、德国全球与地区问题研究所、柏林社会科学研究中心、媒体与传播政策研究所，了解德国智库的运营情况。

2014 年 7 月 18 日，组织专家研讨会，邀请各领域专家 17 人，讨论来源智库的合理性与评价方法的可行性。

2014 年 7 月 25 日，与浙江省社会科学院副院长葛立成交流智库建设、智库评价等有关问题。

2014 年 9 月 2 日，与清华大学公共管理学院教授朱旭峰就"中外思想库建设"进行座谈。

2014 年 9 月 3 日，"全球核心智库评价项目部"更名为"机构评价项目部"。

2014 年 10 月 15 日，赴宁夏社会科学院调研，与张少明副院长等人交流期刊评价与智库评价问题。

2014 年 10 月 21—22 日，赴中国社会科学院欧洲研究所进行智库评价预调查。

2014 年 10 月 23 日，赴中国社会科学院西亚非洲研究所进行智库评价预调查。

2014 年 10 月 24 日，赴中国社会科学院亚太与全球战略研究院、世界经济与政治研究所进行智库评价预调查。

2014 年 10 月 27 日，与中央党校座谈。

2014 年 10 月 27 日，与美国智库专家詹姆斯·麦甘进行会谈，双方互相介绍了各自的评价方法和项目进展。

2014 年 10 月 28 日，赴中国社会科学院俄罗斯东欧中亚研究所、日本研究所进行智库评价预调查。

2014 年 10 月 30 日，赴中国社会科学院拉丁美洲研究所进行智库评价预调查。

2014 年 11 月 9—12 日，赴广西社会科学院、广西区委党校调研。

2014 年 11 月 9—14 日，赴厦门大学台湾研究院、宏观经济研究中心、会计发展研究中心、东南亚研究中心，福建省社会科学院调研。

2014 年 12 月 3 日，赴清华—布鲁金斯公共政策研究中心调研。

2014 年 12 月 10 日，组织研讨会，与国内智库研究专家就智库评价的概念和方法进行探讨。

2014 年 12 月 11 日，接待韩国经济·人文社会研究会代表团访问，与 14 家韩国政府出资智库代表进行座谈。

2014 年 12 月 20 日，与河北经贸大学校长纪良纲、河北社会科学院张小平主任等交流智库评价与期刊评价等问题。

2014 年 12 月 22—26 日，赴新疆维吾尔自治区社会科学院、新疆师范大学、中共新疆维吾尔自治区委党校、中共新疆生产建设兵团党校调研。

2014 年 12 月 26 日，参加上海理工大学电子商务研究院成立大会，就推进电商智库建设等问题进行交流。

中共中央政策研究室经济局副局长白津夫、商务部外资司巡视员刘作章、工信部政策法规司巡视员李国斌、科技部办公厅副主任胥和平、上海理工大学党委书记沈炜和上海理工大学校长胡寿根等领导出席会议。

2014 年 12 月 28—31 日，赴青海省社会科学院、青海省委党校、青海省行政学院、青海省社会主义学院调研。

2015 年 1 月 5 日，赴中国社会科学院财经战略研究院、城市发展与环境研究所、金融研究所、人口与劳动经济研究所进行调研，了解经济片各所智库建设情况。

2015 年 1 月 6 日，接待科技部办公厅原副主任胥和平并会谈。

2015 年 1 月 7 日，接待中国发展研究院秘书长牟善荣一行，详细了解中国发展研究院的发展历程及作为智库的工作方式和内容。

2015 年 1 月 12—16 日，赴安徽省社会科学院、安徽省委党校进行调研。

2015 年 1 月 21—23 日，参加中国社会科学院国际片年度工作会议，与国际片学者就全球智库评价进行交流。

2015 年 2 月 23—28 日，赴美国考察智库，与对外关系委员会、纽约大学国际合作中心、布鲁金斯学会、传统基金会、卡内基国际和平基金会、美国企业研究所、世界资源研究所、战略与国际问题研究所、城市研究所、加图研究所 10 家智库的负责人及美国智库专家进行座谈，了解美国智库的发展、运营状况。

2015 年 3 月 13—14 日，到河南省社会科学院调研。院长喻新安介绍了近年来该院开展智库建设、着力为地方经济社会发展提供智力支持服务方面的有关情况。

2015 年 3 月 16 日，接待中国军事科学院来访，探讨科研评价及智库评价等问题。

2015 年 3 月 17 日，赴中国社会科学院俄罗斯东欧中亚研究所、亚太与全球战略研究院、西亚非洲研究所调研，了解世界相关地区的智库情况，商讨与各研究所合作进行智库信息获取工作。

2015 年 3 月 23 日，赴中国社会科学院欧洲研究所调研。

2015 年 3 月 25 日，赴北京大学国家发展研究院调研，与副院长黄益平教授等座谈。

2015 年 4 月 2 日，赴清华—布鲁金斯公共政策研究中心调研，与中心主任齐晔教授等座谈。

2015 年 4 月 12 日，与浙江工商大学校长张仁寿等交流智库建设与评价相关问题。

2015 年 4 月 16 日，赴中国国际问题研究院调研，与副院长郭宪纲等座谈。

2015 年 4 月 21 日，赴中国社会科学院美国研究所调研，与所长郑秉文、各研究室主任及智库专家进行会谈，了解美国智库的特点，商讨美国智库评价工作的方法。

2015 年 4 月 22 日，赴中国人民大学重阳金融研究院调研，与信息中心总编辑胡海滨、合作研究部主任刘英会谈，详细了解了该院的运行情况。

2015 年 4 月 23 日，赴中国现代国际关系研究院调研，与院长季志业、业务部门主管及院办同志会谈。

2015 年 4 月 28 日，赴中国国际经济交流中心调研，与经济研究部部长徐洪才会谈。

2015 年 4 月 30 日，赴国家行政学院调研，与培训部副主任陈炳才、办公厅副主任牛献忠座谈。

2015 年 5 月 6 日，赴零点研究咨询集团调研，与零点国际发展研究院研究总监郭维维，北京零点指标信息咨询有限责任公司总经理张慧、副总经理姜健健座谈，了解其《中国智库影响力报告》评价体系及方法。

2015 年 5 月 15 日，项目部办公地点迁至中国社会科学院档案楼。

2015 年 5 月 22 日，赴中央党校与经济学部及进修部等部门老师交流智库评价问题。

2015 年 5 月 30 日—6 月 6 日，赴复旦大学公共管理与公共政策研究国家哲学社科创新基地、国外马克思主义与国外思潮研究国家哲学社科创新基地、美国研究中心、日本研究中心、世界经济研究所、信息与传播研究中心、中国社会主义市场经济研究中心、中外现代化进程研究中心，华东师范大学俄罗斯研究中心、基础教育改革与发展研究所、中国现代城市研究中心、中国现代思想文化研究所，上海财经大学会计与财务研究院，上海外国语大学俄罗斯研究中心、欧盟研究中心、英国研究中心、中东研究所，同济大学德国学术中心、环境与可持续发展学院，上海国际问题研究院，上海市委党校、行政学院，上海社会科学院，上海华夏社会发展研究院，中欧陆家嘴国际金融研究院调研。

2015 年 6 月 1 日，在《中国青年报》发表文章《"大而全"不如"小而精"——如何建设中国特色的专业智库》。

2015 年 6 月 4 日，参加第 34 期当代智库论坛。

2015 年 6 月 12 日，做客和讯网"智库访谈录"，录制访谈"中国智库建设路在何方"。

2015 年 6 月 17—23 日，赴英国、比利时考察智库，与查塔姆社、伦敦大学亚非学院中国研究院、欧洲改革中心、欧盟 40、布鲁盖尔、欧洲之友、欧洲国际政治经济研究中心、国际危机研究小组、艾格蒙皇家国际关系研究所的负责人及专家座谈，了解欧洲智库的运营情况。

2015 年 6 月 23 日，在《人民日报》发表文章《对智库热的冷思考》。

2015 年 6 月 30 日，参加中韩人文交流政策论坛。

2015 年 7 月 2 日，赴国务院发展研究中心调研，与办公厅副主任来有为、办公厅综合处处长刘理辉会谈。

2015 年 7 月 8 日，在"中国网"发表文章《摇摆在商业利益与公共责任之间的日本智库》。

2015 年 7 月 10—13 日，赴日本独立行政法人经济产业研究所和株式会社大和总研调研，围绕日本智库的发展历程与现状以及今后的智库建设等问题，与相关人员进行交流。

2015 年 7 月 13 日，参加"国际问题研究与智库建设"报告会。

2015 年 7 月 14 日，在《财经国家周刊》发表文章《排名智库排行榜》。

2015 年 7 月 17 日，在"中国网"发表文章《从"智库"到"行库"》。

2015 年 7 月 20 日，与南京财经大学副校长乔均，南京市社科联主席、社科院院长、党组书记叶南客，副院长李程骅等座谈，交流智库建设、智库评价等有关问题。

2015 年 7 月 22 日，在《光明日报》发表文章《中国智库建设应破解三大难题》。

2015 年 7 月 30 日，参加"全球治理与开放型经济——G20 智库论坛（2015）"。

2015 年 8 月 6 日，参加亚洲开发银行研究所所长吉野直行学术报告会。

2015 年 8 月 6 日，与安徽财经大学党委书记姜利军，安徽省社会科学院党组书记、院长朱士群等交流智库建设的路径等问题。

2015 年 8 月 11 日，在《中国社会科学报》发表文章《发挥智库公共外交功能》。

2015 年 8 月 25 日，参加中国社会科学论坛——"一带一路"与孟中印缅区域互联互通会议。

2015 年 9 月 6 日，赴瞭望智库调研，与总裁吴亮、编辑总监王芳等座谈。

2015 年 9 月 16 日，赴商务部与新闻发言人、政研室主任沈丹阳就智库建设等问题交换意见。

2015 年 9 月 29 日，与到访的贵州社科联党组书记、副主席包御琨一行就地方智库建设座谈。

2015 年 10 月 19 日，接待来访的山东省社会科学联合会副书记、副主席周忠高一行，交流智库评价与成果评价等问题。

2015 年 10 月 20 日，与上海社会科学院智库科研处调研团座谈。

2015 年 10 月 21 日，与商务部国际贸易经济合作研究院院长顾学明就新型特色智库建设等问题进行交流。

2015 年 10 月 24—25 日，与十余所财经大学校领导交流智库评价问题。

2015 年 10 月 30 日，与来访的加拿大智库国际治理创新中心主席 Rohinton Medhora 座谈。

2015 年 11 月 10 日，召开第二届全国人文社会科学高峰论坛，发布《全球智库评价报告》，与来自中国、日本、德国、阿塞拜疆、韩国、美国的 100 余位智库界人士对智库建设问题进行了探讨。

2015 年 11 月 12 日，与来访的南洋理工大学拉贾拉南国际研究院校友会副主席潘家辉座谈。

主要参考文献

中文参考文献

曹振鹏：《党的知识分子政策关系国运之兴衰——新中国
    60 年来党的知识分子政策演变历程及启示》，《贵州社
    会主义学院学报》2010 年第 1 期。

陈振明主编：《政策科学》，中国人民大学出版社 1998 年
    版。

程永明：《日本智库经费来源渠道研究》，《人民论坛》
    2014 年总第 435 期。

褚鸣：《美欧智库比较研究》，中国社会科学出版社 2013
    年版。

［美］戴维·杜鲁门：《政治过程——政治利益与公共舆
    论》，陈尧译，天津人民出版社 2005 年版。

刁榴、张青松：《日本智库的发展现状及问题》，《国外
    社会科学》2013 年第 3 期。

胡鞍钢：《中国特色新型智库：胡鞍钢的观点》，北京大
    学出版社 2014 年版。

［美］卡尔·帕顿、大卫·沙维奇：《政策分析和规划的

初步方法》第二版，孙兰芝、胡启生译，华夏出版社
　　2001 年版。

李安方：《中国智库竞争力建设方略》，上海社会科学院
　　出版社 2010 年版。

李轶海：《国际著名智库研究》，上海社会科学院出版社
　　2010 年版。

林卡、陈梦雅：《社会政策的理论和研究范式》，中国劳
　　动社会保障出版社 2008 年版。

零点国际发展研究院与中国网：《2014 中国智库影响力
　　报告》，2015 年 1 月 15 日。

刘少东：《智库建设的日本经验》，《人民论坛》2013 年
　　总第 426 期。

马骏、刘亚平主编：《美国进步时代的政府改革及其对中
　　国的启示》，格致出版社 2010 年版。

［英］迈克尔·曼：《社会权力的来源》，刘北成、李少
　　军译，上海世纪出版集团 2007 年版。

宁骚主编：《公共政策学》，高等教育出版社 2003 年版。

上海社会科学院智库研究中心：《2013 年中国智库报
　　告——影响力排名与政策建议》，上海社会科学院出版
　　社 2014 年版。

上海社会科学院智库研究中心：《2014 年中国智库报告——影响力排名与政策建议》，上海社会科学院出版社 2015 年版。

谭维克主编：《建设首都社会主义新智库研究》，中央文献出版社 2012 年版。

唐钧主编：《社会政策：国际经验与国内实践》，华夏出版社 2001 年版。

［加］唐纳德·E. 埃布尔森：《智库能发挥作用吗？公共政策研究机构影响力之评估》，扈喜林译，上海社会科学院出版社 2010 年版。

陶文钊主编：《美国思想库与冷战后美国对华政策》，中国社会科学出版社 2014 年版。

王沪宁：《作为国家实力的文化：软权力》，《复旦大学学报》（社会科学版）1993 年第 3 期。

王辉耀、苗绿：《大国智库》，人民出版社 2014 年版。

王莉丽：《旋转门：美国思想库研究》，国家行政学院出版社 2010 年版。

王佩亨、李国强等：《海外智库——世界主要国家智库考察报告》，中国财政经济出版社 2014 年版。

王曙光、李维新、金菊：《公共政策学》，经济科学出版社 2008 年版。

王志章：《日本智库发展经验及其对我国打造高端新型智
　　库的启示》，《思想战线》2014 年第 40 卷第 2 期。

吴寄南：《浅析智库在日本外交决策中的作用》，《日本
　　学刊》2008 年第 3 期。

伍启元：《公共政策》，香港商务印书馆 1989 年版。

谢明:《政策分析概论》，中国人民大学出版社 2004 年版。

许共城：《欧美智库比较及对中国智库发展的启示》，
　　《经济社会体制比较》2010 年第 2 期。

［美］詹姆斯·G. 麦甘：《2013 年全球智库报告》，上海
　　社会科学院出版社 2014 年版。

张树华、潘晨光、祝伟伟：《关于中国建立国家功勋荣誉
　　制度的思考》，《政治学研究》2010 年第 3 期。

中国社会科学院拉丁美洲研究所编：《全球拉美研究智库
　　概览》（上、下册），当代世界出版社 2012 年版。

朱旭峰：《中国思想库政策过程中的影响力研究》，清华
　　大学出版社 2009 年版。

朱亚鹏：《公共政策过程研究：理论与实践》，中央编译
　　出版社 2013 年版。

外文参考文献

Blackmore Ken：*Social Policy. An Introduction*，The 2rd Edition，New York：Open University Press，2003.

Scartascini Carlos，Pablo Spiller，Ernesto Steiny Mariano Tommasi：*El juego político en América Latina：¿Cómo se deciden las políticas públicas?*，Banco Interamericano de Desarrollo，Colombia，enero de 2011.

Abelson Donald E.：*American Think Tanks and their Role in US Foreign Policy*，New York，St. Martin's Press，1996.

Mendizabal Enrique：*Think Tanks y Partidos Políticos en América Latina*，Primera Edición，agosto de 2009.

Mendizabal Enrique：*Think tanks in Latin America：what are they and what drives them?*，Foreign Affairs Latin America，2012.

Garcé Adolfo，Gerardo Uña：*Think Tanks and Public Policies in Latin America*，Fundación Siena and CIPPEC，Buenos Aires，Argentina，2010.

Gerardo Uña：*Think Tank en Argentina*，*Sobreviviendo a la tensión entre la participación y la permanencia*，Documento de Trabajo, Noviembre de 2007.

Smith James A.: *The Idea Brokers: Think Tanks and the Rise of the New Policy Elite*, NewYork, The Free Press, 1993.

McGann James G.: *Global Think Tanks*, Routledge, 2010.

McGann James G.: *Global Think Tanks*, Routledge, 2011.

Arin Kubilay Yado: *Think Tanks*, Springer VS, 2014.

Marshall T. H.: *Social Policy*, The 4th Edition, London: Hutchinson, 1975.

Weidenbaum Murray, *Competition of Ideas*, Transaction Publishers, New Brunswick, New Jersey, 2011.

Aste Norma Correa, Enrique Mendizabal: *Vínculos entre conocimiento y política: el rol de la investigación en el debate public en América Latina*, Primera edición, Lima, agosto de 2011.

Dickson Paul: *Think Tank*, New York: Atheneum, 1971.

Rich, Andrew and R. Kent Weaver: "Think Tanks, the Media and the Policy Process", Paper presented at the 1997 annual meeting of the American Political Science Association, Washington D. C. , August 1997.

Rich, Andrew: "US Think Tank and The Intersection of Ideology Advocacy and Influence ", *NIRA Review*, Winter 2001.

Rich Andrew： "Perceptions of Think Tanks in American Politics： A Survey of Congressional Staff and Journalists," Burson-Marstellar Worldwide Report, December 1997.

Taylor-Gooby P. Dale： *Social Theory and Social Welfare*, London： Arnold, 1981.

Zhu Xufeng： *The Rise of Think Tanks in China*, Routledge, 2013.

福川伸次『政策形成過程における日本のシンクタンクの役割』,『シンクタンクの動向 2002』, 2002 年。

鈴木崇弘『日本になぜ（米国型）シンクタンクが育てたなかったのか?』,『季刊政策・経営研究』, 2011 年 2 号。

小池洋次『政策形成とシンクタンク‐日米比較を中心に‐』,『シンクタンクの動向 2002』, 2002 年。

小林陽太郎『代替的政策形成機関としてのシンクタンクの役割』,『シンクタンクの動向 2003』, 2003 年。

Global Think Tank Evaluation Report

(2015)

Project leader:

Jing Linbo

Project members:

Wu Min, Jiang Qingguo

Liu Xiaoxiao, Hu Wei, Yang Zhuoying, Shen Jinjian, Ma Ran, Liu Bingjie

Wang Lili, Su Jinyan, Lu Wanhui, Geng Haiying, Yu Qian, Hao Ruoyang,

Yang Fating, Xiang Junyong, Zhang Qingsong, Xu Jingyi, Hao Ming, Li Jun, Wu Bo, Zou Qingshan, Chen Yuanyuan, Feng Shouli, Hou Yixiong,

He Yuqiong, Wang Chunhong, Li Yuying, Suo Jianci, Chen Yao, Lu Shanshan, Zhang Zhang

Wang Limin, Zhou Qun, Li Wenzhen, Yao Xiaodan, Wang Ping, Liu Huachu, Yang Xue, Xue Xiaoying, Zhang Xiaoxi, Chu Guofei, Nan Yingshun

Data collectors:

Yang Min, Zhang Lin, Shao Yanan, Han Xü, Cao

Yuanyuan，Hu Chun，

Lin Zhiwei，Li Shuo，Wang Xiuzhong，Zheng Bugao，Yu Jiaying

Contents

1. The Definition of Think Tank

In the past, the term "think tank" was mostly translated into "ideas base", referring to a variety of ideas making or brain storming organizations. It was also known as "think factory", "outside brain", "brain tank", "brain trust", "consultant corporation", "intelligence research center" and so on.

Initially, a think tank used to be a secret chamber that the United States provided for its defense scientists and military staff to hold discussions on strategic issues during the Second World War.

According to *the World Intellectual Big Dictionary*: "A Think Tank, also known as Brain Bank, is an intellectual group which performs research and consulting for governments, enterprises, companies, associations, generally composed of multi-disciplinary and multi-professional experts."[1]

---

[1] An Guozheng, *The World Intellectual Big Dictionary*, (《世界知识大辞典》), World Affairs Press, 1990, P. 1356.

The *Encyclopaedia Britannica* defines a think tank as an institute, corporation, or group organized for interdisciplinary research with the objective of providing advice on a diverse range of policy issues and products through the use of specialized knowledge and the activation of networks.

In 1971, Paul Dixon published the first book on the formation and development of American think tanks named *Think Tank*, in which he proposed that a think tank is "an independent, non-profit policy research institute". It is a permanent entity with the purpose of providing services for policy-making instead of technology, rather than a temporarily-established research group or a committee to give immediate solutions. [1]

James A. Smith states that "The American planning and advisory institutions known as think tanks—the private, nonprofit research groups—operate on the margins of this nation's formal political processes. Situated between academic social science and higher education on the one hand, and

---

[1]　Paul Dickson, *Think Tank*. New York: Atheneum, 1971.

government and partisan politics on the other hand, think tanks provide a concrete focus for exploring the changing role of the policy expert in American life. " [1]

Andrew Rich, who holds a Ph. D. in politics from Yale University, claims that the think tank is an independent and non-profit organization which provides professional knowledge and suggestions to gain support and influence decision making. [2]

Canadian think tank expert, Donald E. Abelson believes that the think tank is an independent and non-profit organization composed of experts who are concerned with widespread public policies issues. [3]

In China, however, there exists a different understanding about what constitutes an "ideas base" and "brain trust".

According to Baidu Encyclopedia, a think tank, originally

---

[1]   James A. Smith, The Idea Brokers: Think Tanks and the Rise of the New Policy Elite, New York: The Free Press. 1993. P. XIII

[2]   Andrew Rich, " US Think Tank and The Intersection of Ideology Advocacy and Influence", NIRA Review: Winter 2001, P. 54.

[3]   Donald E. Abelson, American Think Tanks and their Role in US Foreign Policy, New York: St. Martin's Press, 1996, P. 21.

called an "ideas base", is a public multidisciplinary research institute made up of experts who, in the respects of society, economy, technology, military, and diplomacy provide advice for decision-makers and produce the best theories, strategies, methods and thoughts. In its strict sense, think tanks are NGOs that are independent of governmental agencies. The main functions of a think tank are to propose ideas, to educate the public and to combine talents. By first forming new policy suggestions based upon research and analysis, and then by publishing books, organizing various activities, and taking advantage of the mass media, etc., a think tank tries to gain the support of both the public and the relevant decision makers.

Some scholars believe that an "idea base" refers to a collective body of conceptual knowledge generated by people in social practice, while a "brain trust" is a group of resourceful advisers participating in political affairs. [1]

---

[1]   Chen Zhensheng, "Thinking upon Chinese Academy of Social Sciences Truly Becoming the Think Tank of the Central Government" ("中央社科院真正成为中央思想库和智囊团的思考"), *The State Research of* 2006 (《国情调研 2006 年》), Zhang Guanzi, Shandong People's Publishing House, 2008, P. 845.

All in all, deciding how to define a think tank has remained a problematic and often confusing process for quite some time. It is difficult to give a uniform definition for these different types of organizations, largely because people still have different viewpoints on what a think tank really is. After exploring the various definitions of a think tank, most scholars have finally reached a consensus—that there is in fact no single, unified model of a think tank.[①] In spite of this, Canadian professor Donald E. Abelson thinks that the mode of operation of think tanks is similar to that of private enterprises. Nevertheless, their ultimate effect is not measured by profits but instead by their influence upon public policy. Think tanks in the United States and Canada are, according to the Income Tax Act and the Internal Revenue Code, registered as non-profit organizations. Given their tax-exempt status, it is not possible for them to publicly support any political party. The traditional distinction between think tanks and other sectors in the policy making community lies in the fact that

① Donald E. Abelson, *Do Think Tanks Matter?* (《智库能发挥作用吗?》), Shanghai Academy of Social Sciences Press, 2010, P. 5 – 6.

think tanks place emphasis on research and analysis. [1]

In conclusion, we believe that a think tank is an organization exerting influence upon public policy making through independent intellectual products. Our definition of a think tank emphasizes:

First, a think tank is a form of organization, rather than a natural person. It is the organizational element of a think tank that makes it different from an individual and individual behavior. Thus, Zhuge Liang, Liu Bowen and other individual masterminds in Chinese history cannot constitute a think tank.

Second, think tanks must produce independent intellectual outputs. Think tanks are professional in producing knowledge, and should be equipped with staff possessing professional knowledge and skills to create new products of thoughts.

Finally, think tanks are supposed to have an impact on the formulation of public policy, which is the core function of a think tank. We believe that its influence upon public policy

---

[1] *The Role of Think Tank in Decision-making*, Boao BBC Workingshop Meeting Minutes, 29, March, 2015.

does not need to be understood as the special tendency of political ideology. For instance, RAND Corporation is not willing to label itself as a think tank. On its official website, it declares that "It is generally acknowledged that the term 'think tank' was first applied to the RAND Corporation in the 1960s. At the time, a think tank was a research institute that came up with new ideas that could influence public policy. One important distinction to note is that while 'think tanks' are commonly thought of as organizations with specific political or ideological agendas, RAND is strictly nonpartisan, and our focus is on facts and evidence. Quality and objectivity are the two core values."

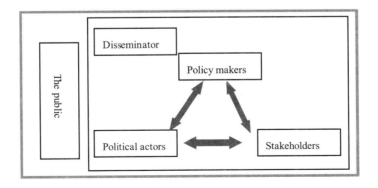

Figure 1　Social Network Structure of Think Tank

Source: by the research group

Policy makers, political actors and stakeholders are constantly communicating with each other. Stakeholders try to obtain favorable policies through directly influencing policy makers' decisions, or indirectly with the help of the political actors who put pressure upon policy makers.

2. The Comparative Analysis of Think Tank Evaluation Methods

People have differing views when it comes to the evaluation of think tanks.

Foreign scholars have made many attempts to evaluate the influence of think tanks. One method is to conduct a quantitative assessment of a think tank's performance by calculating the frequency of media reports and stating opinions to the Legislative Committee. [1]

Based on the analysis of the public awareness of 51 think tanks in America, Andrew Rich and Kent Weaver discovered that it is the think tanks more attractive to media than those bearing ordinary media image that are more likely to be summoned to Congress to state their opinions. [2]

In another study, Andrew Rich finds that the think tanks

---

[1] Donald E. Abelson, *Do Think Tanks Matter?* p. 89.

[2] Rich, Andrew, and R. Kent Weaver. "Think Tanks, the Media and the Policy Process." Paper presented at the 1997 annual meeting of the American Political Science Association, Washington, DC, August 1997.

more frequently reported by the media and that seem to have some relationship with the opinions of policy makers and other opinion leaders are the think tanks that are the most influential. [1]

Furthermore, Donald E. Abelson made a comparison between Canada and America about the opportunities, constraints as well as advantages that think tanks have on influencing policy making.

Scholars in China also conducted an exploration into the influence of think tanks. Beyond the empirical analysis conducted by Zhu Xvfeng on the influence of Chinese think tanks, many researchers and institutes have also made similar attempts.

In terms of the current think tank evaluation methods, both at home and abroad, the following three programs for think tank evaluation have received more attention and triggered debates:

---

[1] Rich, Andrew. "Perceptions of Think Tanks in American Politics: A Survey of Congressional Staff and Journalists." Burson-Marstellar Worldwide Report, December 1997.

2. 1. *The Global Think Tank Report* by the University of Pennsylvania

Since 2006, the Think Tanks and Civil Societies Program (TTCSP) at the University of Pennsylvania has been exploring the evaluation mechanism for global think tanks and has shaped its own unique think tank evaluation procedure. Concretely speaking, every spring they first send emails to staff enlisted in the project database as well as other interested public, inviting them to enter the program website to recommend the candidates qualified for participating in the International Advisory Committee (IAC). Then, the project team will invite the IAC members to nominate the top 25 think tanks of each classification according to their designed categories. The aggregating information about the nominated candidates for top think tanks will be sent to the " Expert Panelists" (EP) who will classify, rank, verify and adjust the institutions filtered by the evaluation indexes provided by the project team and bring out the final ranking of each classification at the end of each year.

Table 2   **The Think Tank Evaluation Index System Used in the**

Global Think Tank Report

Evaluation Index	Concrete Characteristics
Resource Index	Ability to attract and keep leading scholars and analysts; Financial support level, quality and stability; The relationship with policy makers and other policy elites; Ability of staff to carry on rigorous studies and provide timely and insightful analysis; Fundraising capability; The quality and reliability of the network; Key links in the policy academia as well as its relationship with the media
Effectiveness Index	The reputation among medias and political elites of the country; Media exposure as well as the quantity and quality of media citation; Website hits; The quantity and quality of expert testimony submitted to the legislative and administrative agencies; Government briefing; Government appointment; Sales of books; The spread of research reports; Citations in academic journals and public publications; Conference attendance ; The organized seminars
Output Index	The quantity and quality of policy suggestions and innovative ideas; Publications (books, journal articles and policy briefs, etc.); News interviews; The organization of conferences and seminars; The staff appointed as adviser or holding a position getting a post in government
Impact Index	Policy proposals adopted by decision makers as well as social organizations; The focus of network; The advisory role played in political parties, candidates, and transition teams; Awards; The achievements in academic journals, public testimony and policy debates; Publication in or citation of publications in academic journals, public testimony and the policy debates attracted by media; The advantage of list and website; Success in challenging the conventional wisdom; The role in government operation and officials election

Source: from the project team based on relevant documents, see also 2013 *Global Go To Think Tank Index Report* by James G. McGann, pp. 12 – 15.

According to the evaluation's introduction in 2011, the project team invited 6,545 think tanks from 182 countries to take part in the evaluation. Nomination replies were obtained by more than 1,500 individuals of 120 countries, who were requested to recommend the top 25 think tanks of each category in each of the 30 classifications. 25,000 nominations for the 30 categories were received altogether, among which 5,329 think tanks were nominated and 202 were named the world's top think tank. [1]

Starting the research on global think tank evaluation and rankings at an earlier time and continuing to push forward with the project up to now, the TTCSP project team at the University of Pennsylvania has made a landmark achievement in the field of think tank studies. Due to the fact that the "overall impression of subjective evaluation method" adopted by the program is easy to be conducted, thus, as the only full-time staff member, James G. McGann still manages to complete the annual questionnaire survey works with the assistance of internship students.

---

[1]　Wang Jicheng, On the Ranking Mechanism and Influence of McGann's "Global Go to Think Tank Reports" ("麦甘'全球智库报告'排名机制及其影响"), *China Economics Times*(《中国经济时报》),28th,August,2012.

However, at the same time *the Global Go to Think Tank Index Reports* have been widely acknowledged, it cannot be denied that there still exists many problems. After systematically analyzing these historical reports of past years, we hold that these reports hold six major problems.

First, the evaluation method is lacking in objectivity, and should be further improved. As is mentioned above, it is the "overall impression of subjective evaluation method" that McGann adopted for the global think tank ranking. The advantage of this method is that it is easily conducted and evaluation of a large number of objective subjects (global think tank, for instance) can be quickly carried out. Nevertheless, the disadvantage of this method is also very obvious. The outcome could be enormously affected by subjective orientation. The regions and research fields of researchers as well as the opinions they hold, may all exert influence upon the global think tank evaluation and thus affect the accuracy of the evaluation result. We believe that an objective and comprehensive evaluation method for global think tanks requires not only the subjective evaluation, but also lots of multi-level objective indicators for evaluation. Only by combining the subjective qualitative evaluation with the objective quantitative evaluation could we comprehensively conduct a relatively fair and objective evaluation for the global think tanks.

Second, the research strength needs to be enriched. Obviously, to assume a large program such as the global think tank evaluation it must possess a relatively stable financial support and a team made up of personnels qualified for scientific research. In particular, the "overall impression of subjective evaluation method" used by McGann demanded excellent researchers to maximize the removal of deviation in the subjective evaluation so as to ensure the effective implementation of this method. However, it is a pity that this evaluation project conducted by McGann was in his sole charge as the only full-time staff member. Such tasks as data collection, research and analysis were not based on fieldwork or conducted by specialized staff, but rather the internship students from the University of Pennsylvania and other colleges in Philadelphia who had neither received strict academic training nor had acquired sufficient understanding of global think tanks. Some of these students only regarded the project as a summer internship to gain research experience. Thus, it is disturbing to see the quality of research conducted by them.

Third, the expert selection mechanism needs to be standardized and more transparent. As can be seen from McGann's report, the formation of expert group is the most important part of the ranking work. In 2011, through a democratic election for IAC and EP candidates on the internet platform, McGann absorbed the panel members of varied research fields from various regions, the interdisciplinary journalists and scholars, current and former think tank persons-in-charge, think tanks donators, the representatives of the social public, and other think tank-related personnel in order to form the expert group. However, McGann did not give concrete information about their professional fields, regions, positions and technical titles of the EP. For instance, how many members from the Asian regions had taken part in the IAC and EP remain unknown. The composition of the expert members directly determined the cognitive familiarity to the regional thinks tanks selected as the investigation samples. In an email, McGann clearly told these evaluation experts that their selection and ranking work will be ctrictly kept confidential. Meanwhile, he also proposed that if they felt they did not have sufficient time to rank all of the think tanks, they could alternatively spend just a few minutes ranking only the think tanks within their own regions or their professional fields. This random selection and evaluation requirement shows that the quality control of the project was too hasty and sloppy.

Fourth, many loopholes in the report exist that make it questionable and unconvincing. For example, in 2009 the Economics Department at Massachusetts Institute of Technology was ranked 2nd among the top 10 in the category of science and technology, while it never appeared in this category at all in the following years' reports. As early as 2010, the European scholars had systematically cleared up the contradiction about the partial European think tanks in the ranking list of the reports. For instance, the Amnesty International of England was ranked 12th among the Western

Europe Top 40, while it was ranked the 5th among the World's Top 10 (non U. S.); the Friedrich Ebert Foundation of Germany was ranked ahead of the Amnesty International among the Western Europe top 40 but barely appeared on the World's Top 10 list. In this regard, there were as many as 20 such points of inconsistency. Yet another example can be seen in the 2012 report, in which the Institute of World Economics and Politics, an institute affiliated with the Chinese Academy of Social Sciences, were ranked as two separate entities, indicating a lack of awareness of the subordinate relation between the incorrectly presumed-to-be two separate entities.

Fifth, their work attitude is not rigorous enough. Within a ten day period in 2010, three different versions of the report were published (on the 21st, 25th, and 31st of January). Some scholars pointed out that in the first version, the Economic Commission of Latin American and the Caribbean of Chile was ranked the first in Latin America and the Caribbean. However, in the latter two versions, it never appeared on the top 40 list at all. Moreover, it happened that one institution appeared two times within the same table. A similar mistake was also found in the 2014 *Global Go to Think Tank Report*, in which the Development Research Center of the State Council of China was simultaneously ranked 48th and 99th among the top 150 global think tanks. Such large, obvious mistakes expose that their work lacked due attention and appropriate attitude. What is more puzzling is that the Brookings Institution was ranked 2nd amongst the top 70 of the environment group in 2012, while the website of Brookings declared that they do not pay attention to the studies of environmental policy. Similar phenomenon occurred for several years as the institution was ranked in the top 10 in several classification rankings despite their lack of research activities in these fields.

Sixth, *the Global Go to Think Tank Reports* did not win the worldwide acceptance as the media claims. In 2015, it was alleged in the news that *the Global Go to Think Tank Reports* was the result based on the nomination of thousands of international experts and scholars, produced according to scientific and systematic standards. Since 2007, when the global think tank ranking was released, it gradually became the international wind indicator reflecting the performance and comprehensive influence of global think tanks. However, our interviews of famous American think tanks presented different points of view. The Brookings Institution of course was pleased to be assessed as "the global No. 1 think tank" in the report by McGann and vigorously broadcasted the result on their website. However, our investigation and survey showed that the Carnegie Endowment for International Peace, American Enterprise Institute, the Center for Strategic and International Studies, Foreign Relations Committee or the Heritage Foundation and World Resources Institute do not approve or recognize that the Brookings Institute should be awarded as "the global No. 1 think tank". They could only accept the evaluation when they were assessed as No. 1 in certain classifications by McGann.

All in all, we think *the Global Go to Think Tank Reports* by McGann carried the above aforementioned problems, which poses a challenge to its authority. However, much of the Chinese media did not report this objectively, and some scholars and institutes even blindly followed the hype. We suppose that this kind of report must be treated carefully and cannot be overestimated.

2. 2. The *China Think Tank Reports* by Shanghai Academy of Social Sciences

On January 22, 2014, the Shanghai Academy of Social Sciences issued the first *China Think Tank Report* and released the Chinese think tank influence ranking list which included three ranking categories: comprehensive influence, system influence, and professional influence. In light of McGann's "subjective evaluation method of overall impression", this project evaluated our think tanks from four main respects. See details in the table below:

Table 2 **The Evaluation Criteria for the Impact of Think Tanks in China**

Aespects to be evaluated	The specific characteristics
Think tank development and marketing capability	The establishment time and period of existence; Research budget; Ability to retain elite experts and researchers; Channels of cooperation and communication with similar institutions home and abroad

contd.

Aespects to be evaluated	The specific characteristics
Impact on policy-making (core)	Number of times and levels of research products the leaders made comments on; Number of times and levels of think tank experts participating in policy consulting; Number of times and levels of think tank experts invited to provide training for policy makers; The percentage of think tank staff nominated to official posts and staff who used to work for government agencies (the revolving door mechanism)
Academic (central) impact	Quantity of research papers published or reprinted in domestic and overseas core academic journals; Number of times and levels of think tank staff invited to participate in academic conferences at home and abroad; Books and conference papers openly published; Serial research reports openly published
Social (marginal) impact	Frequency of think tank experts expressing views or being reported in the media; Frequency of think tank experts interviewed by media; Website construction, including the number of Web Media such as blogs and microblogs owned by think tank experts; The humanistic care of think tank researches about the vulnerable people carrying policy demands

Source: Think Tank Research Center of Shanghai Academy of Social Sciences, *The Chinese Think Tank Reports of* 2013—*Influence Ranking and Policy Recommendation*(《2013 年中国智库报告——影响力排名与政策建议》),Shanghai Academy of Social Sciences Press, June,2014.

In 2015, the Think Tank Research Center of the Shanghai Academy of Social Sciences modified its think tank evaluation system. The evaluation criteria was built around the influence of decision-making and consultation, academic influence, media influence, public influence, international influence and the ability of development and marketing of Chinese think tanks. It also adopted several rounds of subjective evaluation methods, scored and ranked China's active think tanks from the respects of comprehensive influence, itemized influence, influence with in the internal system, and professional influence. Details can also be seen in the following table:

Table 3   **The Evaluation Criteria of the Impact of Think Tanks in China**

Aespects to be evaluated	The specific characteristics
Impact on decision-making	Number of times and levels of research products leaders made comments on; Number of times and levels of think tank experts participating in policy consulting or invited to provide training for policy makers; Percentage of think tank staff nominated to official posts and staff who used to work for government agencies (the revolving door mechanism)
Academic impact	Quantity of research papers published or reprinted in domestic and overseas core academic journals; Number of times and levels of think tank staff invited to participate in academic conferences at home and abroad; Books, conference papers and serial research reports openly published
Media influence	Ability to guide public opinion of the media; Frequency of think tank experts expressing views in the media or being reported and interviewed by it; Website construction, including the number of Web media such as blogs and microblogs owned by think tank experts
Social impact	Ability to guide public awareness; The humanistic care and action effect of researches about the vulnerable people carrying policy demands

contd.

Aespects to be evaluated	The specific characteristics
International influence	International recognition and international reputation; Frequency of cooperation and communication with similar institutions at home and abroad; Constant attention to major international events and the ability to analyze them
The capability of development and marketing	The establishment time and having long period of existence; Research budget; Ability to retain elite experts and researchers;

Source: Think Tank Research Center of Shanghai Academy of Social Sciences, *The Chinese Think Tank Reports of* 2014 – *Influence Ranking and Policy Recommendation* (《2014 年中国智库报告——影响力排名与政策建议》),January, 2015.

The Think Tank Research Center of Shanghai Academy of Social Sciences believes that the impact of a think tank is a comprehensive embodiment of its impact on decision-making, academic influence, media influence, social impact, as well as its international influence. Thus, only by combining the entire set of channels and mechanisms prompting said influence an evaluation criteria be composed for the impact of Chinese think tanks. Meanwhile, considering that influence was a subjective evaluation and varied because of different persons, perspectives and matters, it was hard to measure with concrete indicators. Thus, the project team mainly used the several rounds of subjective evaluation and the relatively vague ordinal ranking and referred to individual quantitative indicators to conduct evaluation for the impact of think tanks.

The Shanghai Academy of Social Sciences initiated the think tank evaluation in China, being the first to put out the think tank evaluation reports and clearly propose their own indicator system for the evaluation of the impact of think tanks.

The Shanghai Academy of Social Sciences made the classification analysis upon Chinese think tanks. They classified them into the four think tank categories of Party, Politics and Army, Academy of Social Sciences, Colleges and Universities, and Private think tanks. Furthermore, they made a comparative analysis about the nature, form of organization, financial resources and research directions of each category. [1]

It is worth noting that the Shanghai Academy of Social Sciences, according to the classified evolution and research

---

[1] The Think Tank Research Center of Shanghai Acedemy of Social Science, 2014 *The Chinese Think Tank Report—Influence Ranking and Policy Recommendation*(《2014 年中国智库报告——影响力排名与政策建议》), Shanghai Academy of Social Sciences Press, June,2014, p. 9.

fields of Chinese think tanks in the 2013 report, designed 3 categories of ranking. The first category is comprehensive influence, the second is systematic influence, and the third is professional influence.

The problems existing within the China think tank reports by the Shanghai Academy of Social Sciences are:

First, the definition of think tanks needs to be further clarified. As the report put it that, with regard to the selection of think tanks of colleges and universities, it will take the universities as the unit in evaluating comprehensive influence and systematic influence. But for the evaluation of professional influence, the secondary colleges and universities' research centers (related subordinates) were included as units. How exactly to define the think tanks of colleges and universities needs to be further discussed, which involves the question of the quantity and scale of think tanks. [1]

Second, a more critical problem is that the evaluation

---

[1] The Think Tank Research Center of Shanghai Acedemy of Social Science, 2014 *The Chinese Think Tank Report—Influence Ranking and Policy Recommendation*(《2014 年中国智库报告——影响力排名与政策建议》), Shanghai Academy of Social Sciences Press, June,2014, p. 43.

method needs to be improved. The subjective evaluation method of "Nomination + Evaluation + Ranking" adopted by the Shanghai Academy of Social Sciences should be gradually revised to be the "Subjective + Objective" method. [1]

Of course, the transparencies of the evaluation process as well as the set of evaluation weights were more important. For instance, the persons participating in the questionnaire inquiry and the equilibrium of the composition of the evaluation experts, geographical distribution and disciplinary distribution all played an important role in the final evaluation result and should therefore be disclosed. Even if the subjective evaluation method was adopted, for instance, the weight of the evaluation index is supposed to be explained. This is especially the case when considering the scores of the think tanks in the ranking list for the evaluated think tanks to let them figure out their merits and demerits. The currently simple ranking list can neither serve the function of making

---

[1] The Think Tank Research Center of Shanghai Acedemy of Social Science, 2014 *The Chinese Think Tank Report—Influence Ranking and Policy Recommendation*(《2014 年中国智库报告——影响力排名与政策建议》), Shanghai Academy of Social Sciences Press, June,2014,p. 42 –43.

relevant think tanks realize their own deficiencies nor to allow a fair judgment on the evaluation result.

2. 3. The Think Tank Evaluation by Horizon Research Consultancy Group and China Network

On January 15, 2015, the Horizon Research Consultancy Group and China Network jointly released the 2014 *Chinese Think Tank Influence Report*. Four categories of influence indicators were adopted: the professional influence, the influence upon government, social influence, and international influence. And anywhere from 3 to 5 objective indicators were set for each category of influence as shown in the following table:

Table 4   **the Evaluation Indicators for Chinese Think Tank Influence**

Evaluation indicators	Concrete indicators
Professional influence	Quantity and degree of internationalization of the research talents of think tanks; Quantity of articles of the researchers published in academic journals; Quantity of the published books of researchers; Quantity of journals published

contd.

Evaluation indicators	Concrete indicators
Impact on government	Quantity and levels of think tank experts invited to provide training for government staff; Quantity and levels of government entrusted projects; Quantity and levels the leaders made comments; Quantity and levels of think tanks participating in government conferences
Social influence	Search volume of the think tank being searched on the internet; Number of times of the think tank being reported by domestic mainstream media; Number of followers the think tank and its persons in charge have on new medias
International influence	Frequency and ways of the cooperation between the think tank and international organizations; Quantity of foreign think tanks collaborating with the think tank; Number of times of key researchers speaking in international forums; Number of times of the think tank being reported by foreign medias; Numbers of overseas branches

Source: Horizon Research Consultancy Group and China Network, 2014 *Chinese Think Tanks Influence Report*, 15, January, 2015.

Every secondary indicator in the data collection process may be subdivided into more detailed ones according to the actual situation. For example, the researchers may be subdivided into domestic and overseas.

In order to guarantee the research yields more objective results, the Horizon Research Consultancy Group and China Network regard the rankings by the Shanghai Academy of Social Sciences as the first grade indicators. It then converts it to scores which will be combined with the values obtained by the objective indicators, which then finally enable a score of think tanks to be calculated. The formula can be presented as follows:

Think tank's score = (scores from objective indicators × 70%) + (scores from subjective indicators × 30%)

It can be seen that the think tank scores for ranking were weighted more heavily on the objective indicators than the subjective indicators. The Horizon Research Consultancy Group and China Network are expected to build a system completely composed of quantitative indexes which still has a long way to go. And the proportion of subjective scores will be reduced year by year until finally being removed completely.

In terms of the 2014 *Chinese Think Tanks Influence Report* by the Horizon Research Consultancy Group and China Network, firstly, the operation mode for think tank evaluation is innovative. One of its merits is the cooperation with private institutes and the media. Secondly, they try to improve the evaluation method and create the subjective and objective combination evaluation method with the evaluation result of the

Shanghai Academy of Social Sciences as the source data. Nevertheless, it neither discloses the final scores of the relevant think tanks, nor completely presents the quantitative process, which means a lack of transparency. In particular, it does not give a clear definition of think tanks and also did not make the objective data of think tanks as well as their scores known to the public. In the communications with the staff of the Horizon Research Consultancy Group during our field research, they also admitted that many problems still existed during the collection of data given that both the number of people and time devoted to the data collection were insufficient and that experts consulted in the evaluation process were not that representative.

3. The AMI Index System for Comprehensive Evaluation of Global Think Tanks

The index system for comprehensive evaluation of global think tank mainly evaluates think tanks on three main levels: Attractive Power, Management Power and Impact Power. The concrete evaluation model is shown in figure 2.

Attractive Power: the external environment of a think tank. A favorable external environment can attract more resources and enhance the attraction to the evaluation object.

Management Power: the ability of managers to manage and develop a think tank.

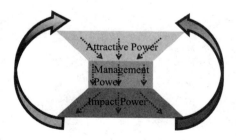

Figure 2　**The Comprehensive Evaluation Model for Global Think Tanks**

Source: from the project team

Impact Power: the direct expression of a think tank and the ultimate embodiment of the two aforementioned powers.

3. 1. The Index System for Comprehensive Evaluation of Global Think Tanks

The comprehensive evaluation index system is made up of five class indicators. This amounts to a total value of 355 points, in which the first-class indicator, "Attractive Power" represents 105 points; "Management Power" represents 70 points and "Impact Power" represents the remaining 180 points.

Table 5 **The Comprehensive Evaluation Index System for Global Think Tanks**

First level indicators	Second level indicators	Third level indicators	Fourth level indicators	Fifth level indicators
Attractive power	Reputation attraction	Decision reputation	Rewards received by institution or staff from international or national government, industry and organization	

contd.

First level indicators	Second level indicators	Third level indicators	Fourth level indicators	Fifth level indicators
Attractive power	Reputation attraction	Academic reputation	Reports, essays and works by institution or staff gaining national prize	
			Researchers' academic morality	
			Academic independence	The independence of research direction and content
				Independence of research conclusion
		History reputation	Founding time	
		Peer review	Expert assessment	
			Third party evaluation	
	Staff attraction	Staff size	Total number of staff	
		Recruitment ratio		
		The ability to attract talents	Work environment	
			Platform provided	
			Personal career planning	
			Payment	Full-time staff's average annual earnings after tax (RMB)
	Products/ outcomes attraction	Research results attraction	Paper downloads	
			Papers reprint amount	
			Website hits	Annual website hits
	Capital attraction	Capital value	Annual R&D spending per capita	
		Capital source	Diversity	

contd.

First level indicators	Second level indicators	Third level indicators	Fourth level indicators	Fifth level indicators
Management Power	Strategy	Development planning		
	Structure	Organization level	Rigor, systematic-ness	
		Independence	Independent corporate capacity	
		CRM (customer relationship management)	The relationship with government, academic institution, media, enterprises and foreign institutions	Full-time public relations practitioner
	System	Information management	Independent website	
		Process management	Rules and regulations	Normalization of establishment and execution
			Strategy and tactics	Harmony
		Outsourcing ability	Translation	
			Data processing	
			Social survey	
	Staff	Quality	Education background of staff	The proportion of the number of staff with Bachelor's degree in the total number of staff
		Structure	Age structure	The proportion of the number of staff aged 30 to 50 to the total number of staff
			Gender structure	The proportion of amount difference between both genders of professionals in the total number of those
		Leader	Reputation	
			Management ability	
		Cooperation ability		

contd.

First level indicators	Second level indicators	Third level indicators	Fourth level indicators	Fifth level indicators
Management Power	Style	Management style	History and tradition Cultural heritage	
	Shared values	Oriented management	Clear values and missions	
	Skills	Professional technical capacity	Educational background of professionals	
			Analysis and decision-making level	
Impact power	Policy influence	The influence upon policy-making	Government commissioned research programs	Amount
			Researchers are invited to teach or to be consulted by governments at provincial level or above	Person-time
			The influence of achievements upon policy	Policy adoption rate
		The relationship with government and decision maker	Revolving door	The proportion of the number of staff once in the provincial office (including temporary) of the total number of staff
				The proportion of the number of staff leaving the agency to the provincial government of the total number of staff
				The proportion of the number of staff taking part-time job in the provincial government of the total number of staff
				The proportion of the number of staff once the officers of provincial government or above of the total number of staff

contd.

First level indicators	Second level indicators	Third level indicators	Fourth level indicators	Fifth level indicators
Impact power	Policy influence	The relationship with government and decision maker	Revolving door	The proportion of the number of staff leaving the agency to be officers of provincial government or above in the total number of staff
			Training for officials	
	Academic influence	Publications	Serials	Amounts
			Reports, papers&works	The amounts of reports and essays openly published by professionals
				The amount of non-public reports submitted by professionals
				The amount of work published by professionals
		Papers cited	Amounts	The amounts of papers citation
		Academic event frequency	Conference	The amounts of workshops, roundtables & forums openly hosted solely or cooperatively
			Academic communication	The amounts of reciprocal visits with other academic agencies within the country
	Social influence	Media exposure	Media exposure of staff	The amounts of policy views reached in national broadcasts, televisions, newspapers & internet
			Media exposure of organization	The amounts of agency reported (including reprinted) by national broadcasts, televisions, newspapers & internet

contd.

First level indicators	Second level indicators	Third level indicators	Fourth level indicators	Fifth level indicators
Impact power	Social influence	Social responsibility	Social public welfare projects	Amounts
		Information disclosure	Open access to researches	
			Website content	Richness
			Website update frequency	
			Research push service	
	International influence	International cooperation	The amounts of workshops, roundtables & forums hosted with overseas agencies	
			The amounts of researches cooperatively distributed with overseas agenciesor personals	
			The total number of staff sent abroad to have academic visits or participate in academic exchanges and seminars	
		Registered branches abroad	Amount	
		Foreign professionals	The proportion foreign professionals	
		Multilanguage	The languages used by professionals to openly distribute reports & papers	Amount
			Language versions of agencywebsite	Amount

3. 2. The Comprehensive Evaluation Index System for Global Think Tanks (the trial version in 2015)

"The Comprehensive Evaluation Index System for Global Think Tanks (the trial version in 2015) " (" hereinafter referred to as 2015 Trial Version of Evaluation Index System") is designed to evaluate global think tanks as well as to further test the scientific value and applicability of the comprehensive evaluation index system. It is the subclass of the Comprehensive Evaluation Index System of Global High-end Think Tank, whose indicators are selected by relevance and reliability. In total it values 283 points with the first class index " attractive power" reaching 82 points, "management power" 51 points and "impact power" 150 points, altogether 72 points less than those of the whole evaluation index system.

Table 6   **The Comprehensive Evaluation Index System for Global**

Think Tanks (**trial version in** 2015)

First level indicators	Second level indicators	Third level indicators	Fourth level indicators	Fifth level indicators
Attractive power	Reputation attraction	Academic reputation	Academic independence	The independence of research direction and content

contd.

First level indicators	Second level indicators	Third level indicators	Fourth level indicators	Fifth level indicators
Attractive power	Reputation attraction	Academic reputation	Academic independence	The independence of research conclusion
		History reputation	Founding time	
		Peer review	Expert assessment	
			The third party evaluation	
	Staff attraction	Staff size	Total number of staff	
		Recruitment ratio		
		The ability to attract talent	Payment	Full-time staff's average annual earnings after tax (RMB)
	Products/ outcomes attraction	Research results attraction	Website hits	Annual website hits
	Capital attraction	Capital value	Annual R & D spending per capita	
		Capital source	Diversity	
Management power	Strategy	Development planning		
	Structure	Independence	Independent corporate capacity	
		CRM (customer relation management)	The relationship with government, academic institution, media, enterprises and foreign institutions	Full-time public relations practitioner
	System	Information management	Independent website	
		Outsourcing ability	Translation	
			Data processing	
			Social survey	

contd.

First level indicators	Second level indicators	Third level indicators	Fourth level indicators	Fifth level indicators
Management power	Staff	Quality	Education background of staff	The proportion of the number of staff with bachelor's degree of the total number of staff
		Structure	Age structure	The proportion of the number of staff aged 30 to 50 of the total number of staff
			Gender structure	The proportion of amount difference between both genders of professionals of the total number of staff
	Shared values	Oriented management	Clear values and missions	
	Skills	Professional technical capacity	Educational background of professionals	
Impact power	Policy influence	The influence upon policy-making	Government commissioned research programs	Amount
			Researchers are invited to teach or to be consulted by governments at provincial level or above	Person-time
		The relationship with government and decision maker	Revolving door	The proportion of the number of staff once in the provincial office (including temporary) of the total number of staff
				The proportion of the number of staff leaving the agency to the provincial government of the total number of staff

contd.

First level indicators	Second level indicators	Third level indicators	Fourth level indicators	Fifth level indicators
Impact power	Policy influence	The relationship with government and decision maker	Revolving door	The proportion of the number of staff taking part-time job in the provincial government of the total number of staff
				The proportion of the number of staff once the officers of provincial government or above of the total number of staff
				The proportion of the number of staff leaving the agency to be officers of provincial government or above of the total number of staff
			Training for officials	
	Academic influence	Publications	Serials	Amounts
			Reports, papers & works	The amounts of reports and essays openly published by professionals
				The amounts of non-public reports submitted by professionals
				The amounts of works published by professionals
		Academic events frequency	Conference	The amounts of workshops, roundtables & forums openly hosted (solely or cooperatively)
			Academic communication	The amounts of reciprocal visits with other academic agencies within the country

contd.

First level indicators	Second level indicators	Third level indicators	Fourth level indicators	Fifth level indicators
Impact power	Social influence	Media exposure	Media exposure of staff	The amounts of policy views reached in national broadcasts, televisions, newspapers & internet medias
			Media exposure of organization	The amounts of agency reported (including reprinted) by national broadcasts, televisions, newspapers & internet medias
		Social responsibility	Social public welfare projects	Amounts
		Information disclosure	Open access to researches	
			Website content	Richness
			Website update frequency	
			Research push service	
	International influence	International cooperation	The amounts of workshops, roundtables & forums hosted with overseas agencies	
			The amounts of researches cooperatively distributed with overseas agenciesor personals	
			The total number of staff sent abroad to have academic visits or participate in academic exchanges and seminars	
		Registered branches abroad	Amounts	
		Foreign professionals	The proportion of the number of foreign professionals in the total number of those	

contd.

First level indicators	Second level indicators	Third level indicators	Fourth level indicators	Fifth level indicators
Impact power	International influence	Multilanguage	The languages used by professionals to openly distribute reports&papers	Amount
			Language versions of agencywebsite	Numbers

3. 3 The Characteristics of the Comprehensive Evaluation Index system for Global Think Tanks

The main characteristics are as follows:

1. The combination of qualification and quantification features, makes a remarkable difference from the think tank evaluation method previously used. Based on the existing methods, it is understood that we should break through the bottle neck of evaluation based on subjective qualification, so as to construct the comprehensive evaluation index system which combines qualification with quantification.

2. The system design suits the working process of think tanks, which conducts evaluation from the three levels of attractive power, management power as well as impact power. The first level is like a funnel, showing the external reputation

of a think tank and its capability of attractiveness; the second level serres as an incubator, fulfilling the role of internal operating capacity of a think tank; the third level bears the resemblance of a trumpet, indicating such capacity of a think tank as international communication and policy impact. The three levels are interactive and the larger the impact power is, the more profound the attractive power is. Meanwhile, the increase of attractive power will support gathering more talents to a think tank, consequently promoting its management power.

3. The wide coverage. The attractive power covers reputation attraction, staff attraction, products/outcomes attraction and capital attraction; the management power according to the theory of 7S, includes strategy, structure, system, staff, style, shared value as well as skills; the impact power incorporates policy influence, academic influence, social influence and international influence.

4. The ability to access experts groups and relevant third parties, which not only develops the function of experts review, but also pays attention to the assessing results of the

third party. The value of the former reaches up to 40 points and that of the latter to 10 points, which altogether occupies more than half of 82 points of the attractive power in the whole 2015 evaluation system, which then reflects the emphasis placed on peer review.

4. The Global Think Tank Ranking and the Evaluation Process

4.1. The Global Think Tank Evaluation Process

4.1.1. The Research Process

(a) Define the source of think tanks

The project team, by synthesizing the existing think tank evaluation results and using internet as well as relative documents, preliminarily collected and grasped the basic information of global think tanks. They also invited the experts of various disciplines to recommend the important think tanks of their own fields. On the basis of bearing a general understanding of the characteristics of global think tanks, they made a definition on think tank in order to narrow the scope of the source of think tanks.

(b) Revise the scope of source of think tanks

Expert consultation as well as fieldwork is core notions of the project. The team invited the specialists from home and abroad to discuss think tanks, social statistics and information management and relevant evaluation systems. Moreover, taking along with them the think tank questionnaires as well as the expert questionnaires, they visited many domestic and overseas think tanks and, according to the feedback information from consultation and fieldwork, made additions and deletions to the source of think tanks and finally confirmed 1787 source think tanks.

(c) Release the expert evaluation questionnaires and think tank questionnaires

To widen the scope of subject evaluation body, the project team identified a large number of experts. On the basis of the research content of think tanks (region + professional field), the project team classified them into 39 categories and looked for the experts conducting assessment for each category who covered varied professions from the world's major countries and regions. 20162 expert questionnaires were in total released.

Meanwhile, regarding the objective evaluation data, the project team tried to establish direct contact with all the source of think tanks through emails, phones and field visits. Among the 1575 think tanks that accepted the questionnaires, 156 replied and 43 were not willing to take part in the evaluation. 359 out of 1781 source think tanks were selected as the most influential think tanks. If these 360 think tanks did not return their questionnaires, the team would gather the information by themselves in order not to leave them out.

(d) Data statistics

The project team, through earnestly and systematically recording and arranging the large number of feedback information of think tanks as well as the expert evaluation and suggestions, gathered the information of key think tanks not returning questionnaires. This was the basis to setting up the global key think tank database and the think tank expert database which ultimately determined the score calculation on the 359 think tanks according to the evaluation index and index weight.

4. 1. 2. Research Method

(a) The collection of first hand material

Field research

The project team had successively launched the on-thespot investigation into more than a hundred key think tanks from the U. S. , Britain, Germany, Belgium, Japan as well as China and had discussions with the person-in-charge of these think tanks and researchers. The aim of the investigation was to review the various operation models, research content, opinions output channels as well as the way to influence decision making of these think tanks.

Questionnaire inquiry

The project team, through sending and collecting the electronic and paper questionnaires from experts and think tanks, obtained the expert evaluation and think tanks data as the basic foundation for subjective and objective evaluation.

The telephone survey

Of the think tanks that failed to respond through emails, the project team took the method of telephone survey to give an introduction to the evaluation project, answer their questions, make connection with the persons in charge and send questionnaires to them in order to get the data of think tanks.

Expert discussion

The project team paid much attention to the suggestions of

experts from various areas. In the whole research process, in addition to holding in-depth discussions with think tank experts, the project team took the opportunity to visit think tanks at home and abroad as well as hosting and attending seminars to exchange ideas with the experts of various fields from different countries and listened to their opinions and suggestions on the program so as to continuously make improvement.

(b) The collection of second hand material

Collection via Internet

In the process of research, through public information and database, the project team made full use of Internet resources to collect the information of think tanks and experts as well as the research results which provided important foundation for the implementation and completion of the project.

Books and reference materials

Before the implementation of this project, many scholars and experts around the world have completed research on think tanks from all respects and have written a large number of books. Against their own specific regions, the project team members looked up relevant materials on the areas they are in charge of in order to grasp the situation of think tanks in various regions and then accordingly confirm the source think tanks.

Research reports

The project team carried out careful studies on the think tank evaluation reports issued at home and abroad, learned from their successful research methods and evaluation system and made efforts to improve their advantages.

Brief introduction to think tanks

Based on the information released by the think tank official website, the project team compiled the brief introduction of the global 286 key think tanks in a Chinese version with the purpose of providing the domestic think tank research with more basic information on the thinks tanks both at home and abroad for further study.

3. The Ranking of Global Think Tanks

This ranking list embodies the top 100 think tanks in terms of the total score of AMI. Think tanks from 31 countries/international organizations. Specifically speaking, 18 of them are from the U. S. , 11 from Germany, 9 from China, 9 from Japan, 6 from South Korea, 5 from Belgium, 4 Italy and Britain, 3 Brazil and Chile, 2 from Argentina, and 1 from each of, Holland, Canada, South Africa, Switzerland, India, Poland, France, Finland, Kyrgyzstan, Norway, Sweden, Turkey, Spain, Greece, Singapore, Israel, Azerbaijan, Egypt, Australia, and an international organization.

It should be noted that due to the fact that the Evaluation Center for Chinese Social Sciences the project team is affiliated with the Chinese Academy of Social Sciences, thus, to ensure fairness and objectiveness of the evaluation, Chinese Academy of Social Sciences and its subordinate think tanks were not included in this ranking list.

Table 7   **Ranking of Global Think Tanks**

Ranking	Country/International Organization	Name of Think Tank	AMI	A	M	I
1	United States	Carnegie Endowment for International Peace	179. 56	64. 56	53. 00	62. 00

contd.

Ranking	Country/International Organization	Name of Think Tank	AMI	A	M	I
2	Belgium	Bruegel	178.20	63.20	54.00	61.00
3	United States	Heritage Foundation	175.00	60.00	51.00	64.00
4	United Kingdom	Chatham House—Royal Institute of International Affairs	172.00	64.00	41.00	67.00
5	Sweden	Stockholm International Peace Research Institute	170.00	62.00	51.00	57.00
6	United States	Brookings Institute	169.40	73.40	48.00	48.00
7	Germany	Konrad Adenauer Foundation	169.00	58.00	43.00	68.00
8	United States	Woodrow Wilson International Center for Scholars	168.36	64.36	45.00	59.00
9	China	Development Research Center of the State Council	168.32	51.32	48.00	69.00
10	United Kingdom	International Institute for Strategic Studies	160.00	57.00	45.00	58.00
11	Japan	Japan Institute of International Affairs	157.60	68.60	30.00	59.00
12	Japan	National Institute for Defense Studies	154.82	66.32	30.00	58.50
13	United States	Council on Foreign Relations	153.64	67.64	34.00	52.00
14	United Kingdom	Overseas Development Institute	152.36	57.36	40.00	55.00
15	Japan	Institute of Developing Economies, Japan External Trade Organization	151.56	56.56	35.00	60.00
16	Korea	Science and Technology Policy Institute	151.36	51.36	29.00	71.00
17	United Kingdom	Centre for European Reform	150.64	51.64	46.00	53.00
18	Germany	Ecologic Institute	150.36	54.36	34.00	62.00

contd.

Ranking	Country/International Organization	Name of Think Tank	AMI	A	M	I
19	United States	Center for Strategic and International Studies	150.04	61.04	41.00	48.00
20	Germany	Bertelsmann Foundation	150.00	48.00	34.00	68.00
21	Korea	Korea Environment Institute	149.50	49.00	38.00	62.50
22	Japan	Center for Northeast Asian Studies, Tohoku University	149.32	45.32	42.00	62.00
23	China	China Institute of International Studies	147.80	54.80	36.00	57.00
24	Switzerland	Geneva Center for Security Policy	147.36	44.36	30.00	73.00
25	Germany	German Development Institute	146.40	61.40	42.00	43.00
26	Italy	Italian Institute for International Political Studies	145.36	54.36	33.00	58.00
27	United States	East West Center	145.18	59.68	46.00	39.50
28	International Organization	Asian Development Bank Institute	144.80	64.80	30.00	50.00
29	Italy	Institute of International Affairs	144.36	67.36	41.00	36.00
30	Korea	Institute of Foreign Affairs and National Security	143.68	46.68	31.00	66.00
31	Brazil	Getúlio Vargas Foundation	143.22	49.72	50.00	43.50
32	Germany	Ifo Institute for Economic Research, University of Munich	142.40	56.40	45.00	41.00
33	Japan	Institute for Global Environmental Strategies	142.20	54.20	47.00	41.00
34	Spain	Elcano Royal Institute	142.00	55.00	32.00	55.00
35	China	China Institutes of Contemporary International Relations	141.70	57.20	38.00	46.50

contd.

Ranking	Country/International Organization	Name of Think Tank	AMI	A	M	I
36	Belgium	International Crisis Group	141.64	62.64	41.00	38.00
36	Japan	Tokyo Foundation	141.64	58.64	28.00	55.00
38	United States	Peterson Institute for International Economics	141.00	47.00	36.00	58.00
39	Japan	Research Institute of Economy, Trade and Industry	140.20	53.20	42.00	45.00
40	China	China Center for International Economic Exchanges	139.66	54.16	43.00	42.50
40	France	Foundation for Political Innovation	139.66	51.16	38.00	50.50
42	Canada	Fraser Institute	139.16	54.16	44.00	41.00
43	Greece	Hellenic Foundation for European and Foreign Policy	139.00	62.00	43.00	34.00
44	Japan	Mitsubishi Research Institute, Inc.	138.90	49.40	28.00	61.50
45	Belgium	European Center for International Political Economy	138.64	51.64	41.00	46.00
46	United States	Center for a New American Security	137.00	55.00	37.00	45.00
47	Switzerland	Swiss Peace Foundation	136.60	56.60	45.00	35.00
48	Argentina	Argentine Council for International Relations	136.00	51.00	35.00	50.00
48	United States	Resources for the Future	136.00	56.00	36.00	44.00
50	Norway	Peace Research Institute Oslo	135.36	65.36	23.00	47.00
51	Belgium	European Policy Center	135.00	60.00	33.00	42.00
51	United States	World Resources Institute	135.00	59.00	42.00	34.00
53	Germany	German Institute for International and Security Affairs	134.86	50.36	30.00	54.50

contd.

Ranking	Country/International Organization	Name of Think Tank	AMI	A	M	I
54	Japan	National Institute of Advanced Industrial Science and Technology	134.80	57.80	30.00	47.00
55	Germany	Kiel Institute for the World Economy, University of Kiel	134.36	54.36	45.00	35.00
56	Chile	Center of Public Studies	134.04	46.04	46.00	42.00
57	Azerbaijan	Center for Economic and Social Development	134.00	48.00	29.00	57.00
57	Israel	Institute for National Security Studies	134.00	57.00	38.00	39.00
59	China	Academy of Macroeconomic Research	133.64	45.64	36.00	52.00
59	India	Delhi Policy Group	133.64	55.64	38.00	40.00
59	India	Energy and Resources Institute	133.64	44.64	41.00	48.00
62	South Africa	African Center for the Constructive Resolution of Disputes	133.00	61.00	38.00	34.00
62	United States	Center on Budget and Policy Priorities	133.00	56.00	36.00	41.00
62	United States	Stanford University, Hoover Institution	133.00	58.00	38.00	37.00
65	Turkey	Istanbul Policy Center, Sabanci University	132.64	46.64	22.00	64.00
66	Chile	Corporation for Latin American Studies	132.04	43.04	50.00	39.00
67	China	Chinese Academy of International Trade and Economic Cooperation	132.00	62.00	35.00	35.00
67	Poland	Center for Social and Economic Research	132.00	57.00	42.00	33.00

contd.

Ranking	Country/International Organization	Name of Think Tank	AMI	A	M	I
67	South Africa	South African Institute of International Affairs	132.00	56.00	41.00	35.00
67	United States	United States Institute of Peace	132.00	41.00	50.00	41.00
71	Kyrgyzstan	Central Asian Free Market Institute	131.98	40.48	30.00	61.50
72	United States	Inter-American Dialogue	131.64	56.64	36.00	39.00
73	Italy	Eni Enrico Mattei Foundation	131.00	56.00	38.00	37.00
73	Netherlands	Clingendael Netherlands Institute of International Relations	131.00	65.00	27.00	39.00
75	Belgium	Egmont Royal Institute for International Relations	130.40	58.40	27.00	45.00
76	Argentina	Center for the Implementation of Public Policies Promoting Equity and Growth	130.32	43.32	45.00	42.00
77	Germany	German Council on Foreign Relations	130.20	52.20	42.00	36.00
78	Korea	Korea Development Institute	129.64	47.64	43.00	39.00
79	Brazil	Fernando Henrique Cardoso Institute	129.50	44.00	45.00	40.50
80	Australia	Lowy Institute for International Policy	129.40	51.40	21.00	57.00
81	Singapore	Institute of Southeast Asian Studies	129.36	47.36	35.00	47.00
82	Finland	Finnish Institute of International Affairs	129.20	57.20	36.00	36.00
83	Italy	Euro-Mediterranean Center for Climate Change	129.00	54.00	42.00	33.00

contd.

Ranking	Country/International Organization	Name of Think Tank	AMI	A	M	I
84	China	National Research Institute, Tsinghua University	128.80	51.80	32.00	45.00
85	Canada	Macdonald-Laurier Institute	128.64	52.64	34.00	42.00
86	United States	Urban Institute	128.04	61.04	37.00	30.00
87	China	National Academy of Development and Strategy, Renmin University of China	128.00	48.00	43.00	37.00
87	Germany	Peace Research Institute Frankfurt	128.00	68.00	27.00	33.00
87	Germany	Potsdam Institute for Climate Impact Research	128.00	56.00	35.00	37.00
90	United States	Institute of World Politics	127.64	47.64	44.00	36.00
91	Korea	Asan Institute for Policy Studies	127.04	48.04	31.00	48.00
92	Netherlands	European Centre for Development Policy Management	127.00	59.00	37.00	31.00
93	Egypt	Economic Research Forum	126.36	52.36	38.00	36.00
94	Chile	Liberty and Development	126.20	45.20	41.00	40.00
95	Brazil	Brazilian Center for International Relations	126.16	46.16	40.00	40.00
96	China	National School of Development, Peking University	125.80	42.80	35.00	48.00
97	International Organization	World Bank Institute	125.54	53.04	33.00	39.50
98	Germany	Friedrich Naumann Foundation for Freedom	125.50	53.00	38.00	34.50
99	Korea	Korea Institute for Curriculum and Evaluation	125.00	42.00	35.00	48.00
100	United States	Rand Cooperation	124.40	58.40	38.00	28.00

5. The Construction of New Type Think Tanks with Chinese Characteristics under the Global Perspective

5.1. The Think Tank Compass

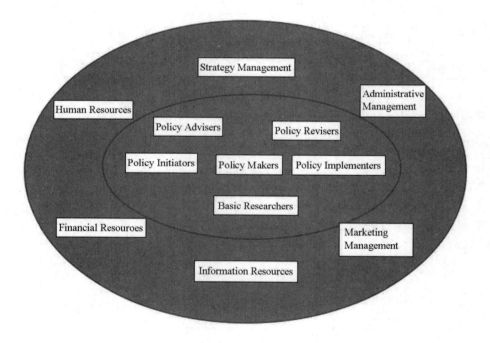

Figure 3　**The Think Tank Compass**

Source：from The project team

We hold that the think tank compass is the core path for

think tank construction. For construction of the base layer of think tanks, the strategic management, administrative management, marketing management as well as the information resources, financial resources, human resources, etc. are supposed to be included in order to consolidate the think tanks foundation; meanwhile, to improve the competitiveness of think tanks, they must have the ability to exert influence upon the related personnel regarding decision making, which includes grounding researchers, policy initiators, policy advisers, policy makers, policy revisers and policy implementers.

5.2. Careful Consideration of the "Fever" for "New Type Think Tanks with Chinese Characteristics"

The Suggestions about Enhancing the Construction of New Type Think Tanks with Chinese Characteristics issued by the General Office of the CPC Central Committee and that of the State Council noted that think tanks are "hot" in China. Whereas, to construct world-renowned new type think tanks with Chinese characteristics, careful consideration was needed.

The "think tank fever" in China was presented in the following respects:

First, fever in numbers—emphasizes increasing the amounts of think tanks, while ignoring their quality. Since the 18th CPC National Congress, General Secretary Xi Jinping repeatedly made important statements on strengthening the construction of new type think tanks with Chinese characteristics from the strategic height of promoting policy-making scientifically and democratically, advancing the modernization of the national governance system and capacity and strengthening of the national soft power. Particularly, the Suggestions released by both offices in January 2015 pushed the think tank popularity to a climax. Some experts claimed that far more than ten thousand think tanks of varieties came into being in the past 2 years.[1] Thus, about five thousand think tanks were estimated to be established. In terms of

---

[1] Chen Yongjie, "To Construct New Type Think Tanks with Chinese Characteristics Needs to Correct Alienation and Prevent Chaos", *Economic Observer*, 25th May, 2015.

amount, the high development speed is striking and the total number had already taken first place in the world. However, it has violated the original intention of the Central Committee in calling for strengthening the construction of think tanks. In April, 2013, General Secretary Xi Jinping with regard to strengthening the construction of new type think tanks with Chinese characteristics made a clear instruction that " as an important part for the nation's soft power and with the development of our situation, the role of think tanks will be more and more important. Thus, the organization and management model for the new type think tanks with Chinese characteristics need to be paid high attention and positively explored. In November 2013, the " Several Important Problematic Decisions about comprehensively deepening reform" made by CPC Central Committee passed in the Third Plenary session of CPC (18) reemphasized the need to " strengthen the construction of new type think tanks with Chinese characteristics as well as establish and improve the decision consulting system". Thus, it is the quality of think tanks that is key. It is only whether or not we can establish and improve the decision consulting system that is the motive and power to enhance the new type think tanks with Chinese characteristics.

Second, Obsession with think tank ramking—focus on the ranking for think tanks while ignoring their integral construction. At the beginning the "Global Go to Think Tanks" issued by Pennsylvania University, it had not much influence either home or abroad, and their evaluation system for think tanks also exhibited many problems. But with the occurrence of think tank "fever" in China, many think tanks concentrated their efforts to ranking, this ranking list then became the target and the project leader McGann was also invited to be the guest for many think tank forums in China. Meanwhile, the Chinese Think Tank Reports respectively released by Shanghai Academy of Social Sciences, Horizon Research Consultancy Group as well as China Network all conducted evaluation upon the influence of national think tanks which recaptured eyes of think tanks upon ranking while ignoring the integral construction of think tanks.

Third, Excessive publicity—paying attention to think

tank publicity, while ignoring the core work of think tanks in public policy studies. It cannot be denied that in the past Chinese think tanks did not attract much attention to the broadcast of their results while lots of research results were laid on the shelf without conducting enough feedback to the relevant decision-making departments, opinion leaders as well as the general public. While making domestic and foreign publicity was an important work for think tanks, it can never be their primary task and while neglecting their core work in public policy studies. Recently, individual national think tanks were keen on media exposure, hosting forums and even seeking popularity by issuing shocking statements or promotions without focusing on advisory research. Such behavior puts "the cart before the horse" as not only did it not cause awareness, but it was enjoyed by other parties and brought about a lot of imitators. If it continues this way, the consequences will be unimaginable.

Fourth, Being quick in following the trend—attaches importance to the tracking of studies on hot issues while taking no account of pioneering innovative research. Think tanks should have their own research directions and characteristics as well as independent opinions about relevant issues. However, nowadays, many Chinese think tanks are enthusiastic about tracking current hot issues which unavoidably creates the embarrassing situation in which thousands of think tanks talking about the same problem. The difficulty of constructing a new type think tanks with Chinese characteristics lies in how Chinese think tanks can control the rights of setting topics for discussion and the rights of speech which certainly demand think tanks to escape imitation and exploit new research fields so as to give real play to the function of politics, consulting and discussion from the height of national interests.

To sum up, the "think tank fever" in China was caused by objective demands and artificial factors. In this great surge, we should not lose our senses. We were supposed to pay close attention to the characteristics of "think tank fever" in order to prevent blindness and impulsion brought by the "dryness-heat" which may destroy the best environment for the development of think tanks. In the meantime, think tank construction needs guidance and should look for truth pragmatism, to go ahead steadily and surely, be quality based and do a good job at basic construction, setting up a problematic orientation and strengthening of policy studies, laying equal stress on internal political consultation and external propaganda, grasping the issues for discussion, bringing forth new ideas on politics, incorporating things of diverse nature as well as developing collaboratively. Only in this way, the Spring of the new type think tanks with Chinese characteristics can be a long one.

5.3. Improving Cultural Soft Power Through the Construction of New Type Think Tanks with Chinese Characteristics

The improvement of our cultural soft power is a requirement of the construction of the new type think tanks with Chinese characteristics.

The word "soft power" was first put forward by Harvard University professor Joseph Nye in 1990. At the time, he published such essays as "Soft Power" and "The Changing

Nature of World Power" respectively in the Journal of Foreign Policy and Political Science Quarterly[1] and on this basis published his work: Bound to Lead: The Changing Nature of American Power.[2] In Joseph's opinion, comprehensive national power included both the "hard power" presented in economics, technology and military and the "soft power" expressed by cultural and ideological attraction in which the former implies the cultural influence, cohesion and appeal of a nation, is the key element for national soft power.

Over the past 30 years since the reform and opening up, our hard power has seen great improvement. First, from the point of economic strength: our GNP ranked seventh around the world in 1980; in 2000, it surpassed Italy, Canada, Spain and Brazil took the sixth place, although it fell back to the tenth in 1990; it overtook France and stood in fifth place

---

[1]　Joseph S. Nye, Jr. "Soft Power", Foreign Policy, No. 80, Twentieth Anniversary (Autumn 1990), Joseph S. Nye, Jr. "The Changing Nature of World Power", Political Science Quarterly, Vol. 105, No. 2 (Summer 1990).

[2]　Joseph Nye, *Bound to Lead: The Changing Nature of American Power*, trans. by HeXiaodong, Beijing: Military Translation Publishing House, January, 1992.

in 2005; it surpassed England ranking fourth in 2006 and exceeded Germany, occupying the third place in 2007. In the second quarter of 2010, it had replaced Japan and reached second in the world. [1]

Then to consider it from the respect of scientific and technological power, the 16th serial report of New China 60th Anniversary issued by the National Bureau of Statistics (NBS) pointed out that for 60 years since the establishment of new China, our scientific and technological power has grown remarkably, the innovation has achieved innumerable benefits and the configuration of social resources has been tilting towards independent research and development year by year. Our total R&D spending following America, Japan, Germany, France and England ranked sixth all over the world. In 2008, the ratio between the whole society's research and experimental development spending and GDP reached 1.52%, increased

---

[1] Jing Linbo, *The Medium and Long Term Trade Strategy of China* (《中国中长期贸易战略》), Beijing: Chinese Social Sciences Press, April, 2015, p. 76.

by 0. 87% over 1991. ① In 2012, the total R&D spending broke one trillion Yuan and the fund input intensity (the ratio between budget devotion and GDP) for the first time exceeded 2% and reached 2. 08% in 2013, increased by 0. 1% over 1. 98% the previous year. All these fully indicated that our scientific and technological power had been constantly strengthened and had narrowed the gap with developed countries such as America and Japan. ②

Finally, in terms of military power. China has a large scale of army forces with 2. 28 million staff for the standing army and 2. 3 million ones for the paramilitary. No matter the ranking by media or the analysis of military experts, and even for the ranking of Defense Weekly of America, our military power was ordinarily ranked in third place all over the world.

① National Bureau of Statistics: "The Ratio Between Our R&D Spending and GDP Reached 1.52%", the Xinhua News Agency, 25th, September, 2009.

② The 2013 *National Science and Technology Investment Bulletin* jointly issued by NBS, Ministry of Science and Technology and Ministry of Finance showed that in 2013, the national total R&D investment reached 1184. 66 billion yuan, an increase of 154. 82 billion yuan and 15% higher than the previous year; the average expenditure for the R&D staff (full time) was 335 thousand yuan, a year-on-year increase of 18000 yuan.

The American Business Insider applying the existing national military databases and mainly taking the famous GFP① ranking list as the foundation published the top 35 world armies. The GFP was one of the most authoritative ranking lists in the world, whose database collected national army information all of the world and made analysis and conclusions. According to the data provided by Business Insider, in order, the world's top 10 military powers were America, Russia, China, India, England, France, Germany, Turkey, Korea and Japan.

However, while our hard power is improving, the soft power has not seen the same great progress, still having lots of shortcomings.

First, in the respect of our core value system, China was

---

① GFP applied a complicated evaluation method to investigate more than 50 factors and according to the calculation results got a score (fire index) roughly reflecting a nation's army power. Meanwhile, to ensure the evaluation as objective as possible, it used mark-adding and mark-reducing system and attached several add-ones mainly including regardless of nuclear weapons, considering the national geographic features, not just conducting evaluation upon the numbers of weapons and equipment, considering the production and consumption of certain resources, not reducing marks if a country without marine outfall lacked navy, mark-reducing for the limitation of naval capability and regardless of the features of national political and military leader. Cited from Iron & Blood(铁血军事): http://bbs. tiexue. net/post2 – 8265750 – 1. html.

still at the edge of the Western discourse system. Because the discourse system construction relatively lagged behind the practice of the Chinese road to riches connotation[1], the value concepts as well as theoretical system that tell the "Chinese Story", objectively interpreting the "Chinese Miracle" and jointly casting "Chinese Dream" needed to be further improved.

Second, regarding the cultural products and services, no matter, mining or utilization of the traditional cultural factors, or developing new cultural products and service with the help of modern technology, there is a big potential in China in finding how to inherit and carry forward the five thousand years of Chinese civilization and how to grasp the opportunities in the new information age needs overall planning and collaborative research.

Third, in terms of micro-foundation, our citizens' overall quality, social morality, professional ethics, family virtues as

---

① Li Tao, Lin Jingwei, the Improvement of Chinese Soft Power: Problems and Approaches (中国软实力提升:问题与出路), *Red Flag Manuscript* (《红旗 文稿》), 9th July, 2013.

well as personal morality all need to improve. It still had a long way to go to have the citizens carry the cultivation matching the magnitude of a great nation so as to achieve the real "State of Ceremonies".

Fourth, regarding the international communication system, the Western power with America as their representative was still mighty and China on the whole was in a passive state in dealing with it. In particular, the "China threat theory" of various versions brought massive negative influence upon Chinese soft power. Thus, turning passive response to active approach and breaking the curse of "China threat theory" need continued efforts.

General Secretary Xi Jinping hosted the 12th collective learning in 2013 for the Political Bureau of Central Committee and pointed out that to improve national cultural soft power concerned the realization of "Two Century Goals" and the "Chinese Dream".[1] At the same time, all these closely associated with the construction of new type think tanks with

① Shen Haixiong, "Harden Our Cultural Soft Power" ("让我们的文化软实力硬起来"), *Outlook* (《瞭望》),2014(2).

Chinese characteristics just because the think tank was the important carrier of national soft power and had become an increasingly key factor for international competition. As General Secretary Xi elaborated, the four aspects of making efforts to consolidate the basis of national cultural soft power are to spread Chinese contemporary value concepts, to reveal the unique charm of Chinese culture and to improve international discourse correctly were not only the fundamental guidance for constructing a socialist cultural power and improving national cultural soft power, but also the actual requirement for building the new type think tanks with Chinese characteristics.

5.4. Establishment of New Type of Chinese Characteristic Think Tanks and Promoting the Modernization of National Governance

As is pointed out in 'Decision of the CCCPC on Major Issues Concerning the Comprehensiv Deepening of the Reform, "The general purpose of deepening its all-round reform is to develop socialism with Chinese characteristics, to advance modernization in the State governance system and governance capability". We consider it fully displayed the governance concept of keep up with the times while addressing the core issue for operating our country. All of them are closely related to the establishment of the Chinese characteristic Think Tank.

First, to comply with the requirement of the global governance, China's Think Tank should have a global vision.

In 1990, Willy Brandt, former president of theSocial Democratic Party of Germany and National Development Council, first proposed the concept of "global governance". In 1991, on the conference held in Sweden, participants of the conference published the " Global security and management proposal in Stockholm", in which they called for the establishment and development of multi-sided regulation and management systems in order to promote inter-dependence and sustainable development on a global scale. In 1992, 28 international celebrities sponsored the Commission on Global Governance. In 1995, at the 50th anniversary of the United Nations, the global governance committee announced a research report named "Our Global Neighborhood". For the first time, it systematically demonstrated the concept of global governance, its value, and the relationship between global governance and economic globalization, also global security. According to the definition given by the "global governance committee", governance is the integration of the various approaches to the management of the common affairs of individuals and institutions, in both public and private sectors. It is a long-lasting process, in which conflicts or multiple interests can coordinate and cooperate with each other. It not only includes formal policy arrangements, but also informal ones. The so-called global governance refers to the situations in which we use international policies with restrictive forces and effective international cooperation to solve the globalized political, economic, ecological as well as security issues (including global conflict, humanity, immigrants, drugs, smuggling and epidemics, etc.), in order to maintain a normal global social political governance order. In accordance with the trend of international governance, China should develop its own global governance theory,

Deepen the analysis of globalization and global governance, correctly understand the essence and rule of global governance, and form China's own globalization and global governance theory according to the characters of our country as well as national interests. Admittedly, the most urgent matter for constructing China's own global governance theory is to construct our own national governance theory and reinforce its foundation. The Think Tanks of our country should actively participate in the issues, giving suggestions and sharing their wisdom of governance.

Nowadays, the global governance issue has gone beyond the traditional political or economic issue, and gradually expands into fields like climate changes and network security. All of them demand higher professional requirements, which urgently require professional Think Tanks to provide corresponding solutions. What's more, in an era when there are both global cooperation and global conflicts, how can China, as a big emerging country, deal with the relationship with developed countries (especially with the US), other BRICS countries and the neighboring countries? Those issues require corresponding Think Tanks to conduct related researches and make long-term and strategic suggestions.

Second, to comply with the demand of China's increasing comprehensive national strength, China's Think Tanks must have the ability to solve problems on every aspect.

In the era of globalization, the competition of comprehensive national strength is the key factor among national competition. Promoting economic development, increasing economic output, improving people's living standards and strengthening national defense are the basic ways to increase the overall national strength. However, in the era of globalization, other elements of national competitions have become increasingly important as well. For example, the level of culture, education, mental and physical fitness, the level of scientific and technological research, the superiority and advancement of national culture, the human resources and strategic talents in the country, the legitimacy and cohesion of the government, the degree of solidarity and stability of the society, the sustainable economic and social development, and so on. We should have a clear mind that in the process of the participation in global governance, economic and military power alone are not enough to effectively safeguard national sovereignty. We must also strengthen the power of morality, politics and judiciary. To comprehensively progress in socialist economic construction, political construction, cultural construction, social construction, ecological civilization construction, to speed up the development of the socialist market economy, democratic politics, advanced culture, harmonious society, ecological civilization, it is required to start from the improvement of the national governance system, reasonable suggestions from various types of Think Tanks are needed.

Third, to comply with the deepening of all-round reform in China, China's Think Tank must strive to solve the current problems.

"The reform of the economic system is the focus of all the efforts to deepen the all-round reform. The core issue is to deal with the relationship between government and the market, so that the market plays a decisive role in the allocation of resources while the government could play a better role. " The ability of governance is reflected by how to coordinate the various interest groups, giving full play to the market and the government in different roles. Take the real estate control policy as an example. The basic principle in the housing demand management is to mainly regulate the demands rather than the supplies. "Supporting demands of basic living, while curbing demands for investment" is the basic policy of real estate the market regulation that must be adhered to. In particular, starting in 2010, more stringent control policies were introduced. These policies were good, but faced many difficulties: the housing properties were difficult to confirm, the standard, uniform recognition of second houses and remote purchases were difficult to grasp and implement. In some extreme cases some people faked divorce to circumvent the property identification of "the second house", resulting in the failure of the relevant regulatory policies. Loan restrictions, purchase restrictions, price restrictions and non-local family restrictions coupled with the property tax pilot, the 20% personal income tax for second-hand housing and other means were all applied. Such severe demand control measures still could not bring about the expected effect, which is indeed worthy of our reflection. It is also indirectly reveals the inadequacy and the inefficacy of suggestions offered by the Think Tanks of China. Control measures focused too much on housing demand, causing the demand to be curbed. What is more, demands for housing were not subdivided and different measures were not taken. A simple regulatory policy cannot have a good handle of diverse needs, failing to distinguish the basic housing needs from speculative demand. The demand-oriented policy in the past was nothing more than an increase of the transaction costs for buyers. For the speculators, they will pass on these costs. For those who have basic needs, especially the low-income class, cannot benefit from this policy at all. In housing regulation, we must avoid the confusion of different situations, and must not confuse with government subsidies and market objectives. Instead, we must also give full play to protections from the government and the market regulation function itself.

In addition, the monetary policies, fiscal policies, even "one belt one road" and other national policies had Think Tanks take the lead. With the deepening of reform, the government has increasing reliance on Think Tanks. We firmly believe that the role of Think Tanks will become increasingly important.

Fourth, to cope with the needs of establishing overall national security strategies, China's Think Tanks must shoulder the responsibility for our national mission.

All countries shoulder their responsibilities for global security, while big countries shoulder more. China bears important obligations not only in the maintenance of peace, the control of military scale, the prevention of the spread of nuclear weapons, but also in the security of global economics, the security of ecological environments and the safety of certain areas. At the same time, the era of globalization is defined by Information and the Internet, thus the content and form of national security has undergone major changes. Information security has become a matter of unprecedented importance. Therefore, China's Think Tanks also must comply with the needs of establishing the national security strategies and must have a new national security concept. At present, China has established the National Security Council to improve the national security system and the national security strategies so as to ensure national security. In addition to maintaining integrity, national dignity and national security outside the territory, we should raise matters, like reducing financial risk and foreign economic dependence, protecting strategic resource reservations, protecting strategic talents, promoting national culture, maintaining ecological balance, ensuring the security of the species, fighting against international terrorism, up to the height of safeguarding national sovereignty and autonomy, which requires China's Think Tanks to keep up with time and offer insights into politics, economy, military, science and technology, culture, education, information, resources, talents, ecology and so on. We should also give positive suggestions in enhancing national capacity to withstand global risks, to ensure the autonomy of the country when actively participating in the global governance process.

5.5. Solve Three Difficulties in Constructing New Think Tanks with Chinese Characteristics

We need to put forth effort to solve three difficult

problems in constructing new think-tanks with Chinese characteristics:

First, Independence. It is well known that independence is the fundamental philosophy that America insists on when constructing think tanks. Nowadays, highlighting the independence of think tanks is the challenge we are facing when creating new think tanks with Chinese characteristics.

Independence is shown in two aspects. One is the independence of finance and the other is the independence of standpoint. As for the former, the majority of think tanks in China are state-funded. It is very hard to turn them into think tanks relying on social fund raising in a short term. For this reason, we can gradually promote the diversification of capital by encouraging nongovernmental capital investment in the construction of emerging think tanks and encouraging social capital to set up related issues. From the respect standpoint, some foreign institutions frequently criticize the fact that sometimes think tanks in China attach themselves to government so they can only interpret policy and can't voice independently. Consequently, think tanks find it hard to play an efficient role of participating in and discussing government and political affairs. Does it really mean think tanks funded by government and affiliated with government can't make an independent voice? For that matter, we need to make bold attempts to, develop new channels and seek new paths. We think related think tanks should be encouraged to put forward independent ideas in the public policy field on thepremise of not breaching party and national policy lest government decision-making departments make wrong decisions in their single way of thinking. Thus, open, inclusive, rational and shared social environment is not only an essential condition of current think tank construction but also an important link of enhancing its independence.

Second, Diversity. Independence and diversity are closely related. Firstly, diversity refers to diversification of types of think tanks. There are not only think tanks with government backgrounds, but also civil think tanks; there are not only think tanks based in scientific institutions and colleges, but also think tanks affiliated with institutions supported by government, professional groups and media organizations; there are not only domestic thinks tanks but also foreign think tanks. Secondly, diversity means there should be different voices and solutions as references for decision makers. Publishing different opinions for different think tanks reflects the advancement of social reasonableness and tolerance as well as diversity. Finally, diversity is relevant to characteristics of think tanks. A single flower does not make a spring. It requires us to pay more attention to unique characteristics of new think tanks in China, concentrating on related fields, training professional teams and developing strengths of think tanks. Think tanks in America lead the way in this respect, for example, Rand Corporation which is good at military research expands its focus area into international studies. Both The International Institute for Strategic Studies in Britain and The Center for Strategic & International Studies mainly focus on foreign policy and are world leading think tanks in the international strategy study area. American Enterprise Institute which has strong links with the Republican Party is an important policy research institution for the American conservative. Many key officials of

Republican Party join American Enterprise Institute which is also called the shadow cabinet and government in exile of the Republican Party. American Enterprise Institute and Brookings Institution are referred to as "Two think tanks" while the former one is also called "conservative Brookings".

Third, discourse power. It refers to dominant discourse power domestically but more importantly, international discourse power. Throughout the development history of think tanks, we can clearly see that holding discourse power, setting new research agendas and guiding public opinion at home and abroad is the essential role of think tank. For instance, since its inception in 1977, Cato Institute deeply influenced by the classical liberalism of Adam Smith advocates reducing government intervention on domestic politics, economy and society as well as intervention on politics and military on the international stage. For this reason, a series of related research agendas and policy advice is always put forward including reducing federal government intervention on market operation and local state government, abolishing minimum wage regulation and corporation subsidies as well as economic trade barriers. At the same time, Cato Institute proposes to deepen the freedom of the school selection system, abolish the racial discrimination policy implemented by government, reform anti-drug policy and so on. In addition, the notion of "G2" and "G3" is elaborately planned by experts from think tanks.

Certainly, we are delighted that we have attained fresh achievement in "the Belt and Road" and "Asian Infrastructure Investment Bank", however, we hope new think tanks with Chinese characteristics can publish more ideas at home and abroad as well as lead global discourse.

5.6. Six Major Relationships to be Dealt with Correctly in the Construction of New Think Tanks with Chinese Characteristics.

We need to deal with six major relationships when building new think tanks with Chinese characteristics.

First, the relationship between basic research and countermeasure research. Basic research focused on by scientific research institutions and colleges aims to answer the question of WHAT and WHY, simplify complicated reality, select critical variables, find out logical relationships between variables and interpret it reasonably. Think tanks pay more attention to countermeasure research which intends to answer the question of HOW. It doesn't only need to surpass basic research but also understand policy. Besides that, countermeasure research aimed at seeking solutions to practical problems can't be done well without rich practical experience and a strong understanding of problems. There is a dialectical and developmental relationship that exists between basic research and countermeasure research which could be deeper and more influential with the good support of basic research. Otherwise, countermeasure research is like water without a source. As a consequence, we should build new think tanks with Chinese characteristics rationally and not confuse the relationship between basic research and countermeasure research. We need to put the same emphasis on both of them in the process of building new think tanks with Chinese characteristics and produce research outcomes which can stand tests of actual practice and history. Only in that way, countermeasure research can be based on solid basic research. We must firmly oppose the eagerness for quick success and instant benefit especially as some institutions propose numerous "ideas" to get temporary attention in very short time.

Basic research and countermeasure research have different emphasis. Within limited financial and human resources, we must deal with the relationship between them. How to make a right choice if we can't get everything? Especially for researchers, it's very difficult to make achievements both in basic research and countermeasure research.

Second, the relationship between scientific research evaluation and think tank evaluation. Basic research concentrates on publishing academic papers and monographs but countermeasure research focuses on advice which has been adopted by government. Their evaluation systems are different and how to balance different evaluation systems in the same institution has become the core issue for constructing think tanks. Initiatives will be fully aroused in constructing think tanks only if we take full advantage of the evaluation system.

Third, the relationship between internal strength and external publicity. Strengthening their own advantages is the core competency for think tanks. Constructing think tanks should be guided by the Basic Principle of Marxism and the Theoretical System of Socialism with Chinese Characteristics and implemented around major issues of economic and social development and international affairs. We should provide intelligence service of high quality for central decision-making and carry out global, strategic, prospective, systematic and comprehensive research as well as produce research outcomes and theoretical perspectives which are very practical, credible and influential. To achieve this goal, we need to keep enhancing our own strengths.

Meanwhile external publicity is also crucial to think tanks, just as the saying goes"the good wine kept in deep auey is not likely to be tasted by the public" Distinguished think tanks in America spare no efforts in publicity for example both Brookings Institute and Carnegie Endowment for international Peace have special departments and staff in charge of promoting outcomes and establishing a network system at home and abroad. In that way, achievements in scientific research can be promoted well through various channels especially in the digital era. All successful experience is worth learning.

Fourth, the relationship between think tank construction and logistical support. Think tank construction can't be done without logistical support. We hold the opinion that a logistics support system should include a data support system, daily administrative processing system, financial system, etc. Firstly, a data support system is the fundamental guarantee for think tanks. With the big data era coming, think tanks in China must think on how to set up large and unified cloud database infrastructures where huge amounts of date can be stored and manipulated in the field of philosophy and social sciences. Besides that, we must think on how to establish a data filtering system by making use of high-volume databases to obtain core data and build effective decision-making support systems. On the other hand, to improve the ability for crises management in government sectors, we should consider how to adapt to the digital age and set up effective online public opinion feedback systems.

Secondly, daily administrative processing system provides strong security for think tanks. Inefficient daily administrative processing has always seriously affected think tanks in a negative way, which can be improved by drawing on advance foreign experience. Currently, researchers in China have to spend lots of valuable time filling-in different forms and dealing with a pile of bills. In other words, they have less time to do research. According to the experience of think tanks in Britain and America, most researches are conducted by one researcher and one assistant. If we follow this model, it would be more effective than the old way we adopted that requires two researchers to jointly finish the research program. Following the research model in Britain and America, research assistants are responsible for providing logistical support, which saves a lot of time for researchers and improves the working efficiency of think tanks.

Finally, financial system is the lifeblood of think tanks. At present, state-funded think tanks haven't felt the financial pressure which independent private think tanks always have.

With the increasing competition among think tanks, the sound and ordered development of think tanks is closely related to financing capacity. In Euromerican developed countries, one of the important duties for leaders in think tanks is raising funds to support their sustainable development.

Fifth, the relationship between being local and being global. New think tanks with Chinese characteristics surely aim to solve the practical problems China faces; influencing Chinese policy, maximizing the national interests of China and fostering the research atmosphere with Chinese the discourse system. We have to realize new think tanks with Chinese characteristics can't blindly follow the development model of think tanks abroad, particularly, we can't allow any act harmful to national interests so we should prevent the tendency of the Americanization of think tanks, avoid the research agendas of think tanks being under another party's control and stop all treasonable acts.

Meanwhile, we need to adhere to opening up and incorporating beneficial things from diverse cultures as well as deepening mutual communication with leading think tanks in foreign countries. On the other hand, we need to make more efforts to go abroad, actively engage in discussions on international affairs and clarify our own points. What's more, we could shape public opinion and set up new research agenda to grasp international discourse correctly.

Sixth, relationship between professionals and interdisciplinary talents. Building professional teams of high quality, interdisciplinary and multi-typed for think tank is very important. High quality means professionals in think tanks should have an international vision, thorough knowledge of the world, and a deep understanding of Chinese conditions and know the domestic policy environment. To be interdisciplinary requires experts with reasonable knowledge structure and multiple skills in different given areas. Multi-type means experts in think tanks must have different working experience in various areas and have good capability of communicating with government sectors. There is a " revolving door mechanism" in American think tanks, which means almost 4, 000 staff members transfer their positons every four years particularly catching the time of the alternation of ruling parties. However, it is beneficial to government and think tanks. Comparatively speaking, there is a lack of staff mobility and exchange between think tanks and government sectors in China, which means staff in think tanks should actively learn about how the government operates. Through this way, the role of participating in and discussing government and political affairs can be fully played.

Bibliography

Cao, Zhenpeng, "The Party's Intellectual Policy is Related to the Rise and Fall of the Country: The Evolution of the Party's Intellectual Policy in the 60 Years of New China and its Revelation", 2010.

Chen, Zhenming, "Policy Science", Renmin University of China Press, 1998.

Cheng, Yongming, "Study on the Sources of Funding for the Japanese Think Tanks", People's Tribune, 435, 2014

Chu, Ming, "A Comparative Study on American and European Think Tanks", China Social Science Press, 2013

Truman, David, "The Governmental Process: Political Interests and Public Opinion", translated by Chen Yao, Tianjin Renmin Press, 2005.

Xi, Liu & Zhang, Qingsong, "The Current Development Situationand Problems of Japanese Think Tanks", Social Sciences Abroad, May 2013.

Hu Angang, "New Think Tank with Chinese Characteristics":

Hu Angang's views, Peking University press, 2014.

Patton, Carl V. & Sawicki, David S., "Basic Methods of Policy Analysis and Planning, Second Edition", Huaxia Publishing House, 2001.

Li, Anfang, "Construction Plan of the Competitiveness of Chinese Think Tanks", Shanghai Social Science Press, 2010.

Li, Yihai, "Study on Famous International Think Tanks", Shanghai Social Science Press, 2010.

Lin, Ka & Chen, Mengya, "Theory and Research Paradigm of Social Policy", China Labor and Social Security Publishing House, 2008.

Horizon China & China Internet Information Center, "2014 China Think Tank Impact Report", 15th January, 2015.

Liu, Shaodong, "Japan's Experience in the Construction of Think Tanks", People's Tribune, 426, 2013.

Ma, Jun & Liu, Yaping, "The Progressive Era of America", Truth & Wisdom Press, 2010.

Mann, Michael, "The Sources of Social Power": Volume 1, A History of Power from the Beginning to AD 1760,

Translated by Liu Beicheng & Li Shaojun, Shanghai Century Publishing Group, 2007.

Ning, Sao, "Public Policy Science", Higher Education Press, 2003.

Think Tank Research Center of Shanghai Academy of Social Sciences, "The Chinese Think Tank Reports of 2013 – Influence Ranking and Policy Recommendation", Shanghai Academy of Social Sciences Press, June2014.

Think Tank Research Center of Shanghai Academy of Social Sciences, "The Chinese Think Tank Reports of 2014", Shanghai Academy of Social Sciences Press, June2015.

Tan, Weike, "Research on the Construction of the Socialist New Think Tank in the Capital", Central Party Literature Press, 2012.

Tang, Jun, "Social Policy: International Experience and Domestic Practice", Huaxia Publishing House, 2001.

Abelson, Donald E. , "Do Think Tanks Matter? Assessing the Impact of Public Policy Institute", translated by Hu Xilin, Shanghai Academy of Social Sciences Press, 2010.

Tao, Wenzhao, "American Think Tanks and Foreign Policy

Toward China After the Cold War", China Social Science Press, 2014.

Wang, Huning, "Culture as National Strength: The Soft Power", Fudan University Journal of Social Science, 3, 1993.

Wang, Huiyao & Miao, Lv, "Global Think Tanks", People's Publishing House, 2014.

Wang, Lili, "The Revolving Door: the Study on American Think Tanks", Chinese Academy of Governance Press, 2010.

Wang, Peiheng & Li, Guoqiang, "Overseas a Think Tank: Think Tank Report – The World's Major Countries", China Financial & Economic Publishing House, 2014.

Wang, Shuguang & Li, Weixin & Jin, Ju, "Public Policy", Economic Science Press, 2008.

Wang, Zhizhang, "The Development Experience of Japanese Think Tanks and Its Revelations for China to Build new Type of High-end Think Tanks", Thinking, 40 – 2, 2014.

Wu, Jinan, "Analysis of the Role of Think Tanks in Japan's Foreign Policy Making", Japanese Studies, 3, 2008.

Wu, Qiyuan, "Public Policy", The Commercial Press, 1989.

Xie, Ming, "Introduction to Policy Analysis", Renmin University of China Press, 2004.

Xu, Gongcheng, "Comparison of European and American Think Tanks and the Revelations to the Development of Chinese Think Tanks", Comparative Economic & Social Systems, 2, 2010.

McGann, James G. , "Global Go To Think Tank Index Report 2013", Shanghai Academy of Social Science Press, 2014.

Zhang, Shuhua & Pan, Chengguang & Zhu, Weiwei, "Thoughts on the Establishment of A National Meritorious Honor System in China", Cass Journal of Political Science, 3, 2010.

Institute of Latin American Studies, Chinese Academy of Social Sciences, "Overview of the Global Think Tanks on Latin American Studies" (Volume 1 and Volume 2), Contemporary World Press, 2012.

Zhu, Xufeng, "Study on the Influence of Chinese Think Tanks in the Policy Making Process", Tsinghua University

Press, 2009.

Zhu, Yapeng, "Research on the Public Policy Process: Theory and Practice", Central Compilation & Translation Press, 2013.

Blackmore, Ken, "Social Policy. An Introduction", The 2rd Edition, New York: Open University Press, 2003.

Scartascini, Carlos, Pablo Spiller, Ernesto Steiny Mariano Tommasi, "El Juego Político en América Latina: Cómo se Deciden Las Políticaspúblicas?", Banco Interamericano de Desarrollo, Colombia, enero de 2011.

Abelson, Donald E. ,"American Think Tanks and Their Role in US Foreign Policy ", New York, St. Martin's Press, 1996.

Mendizabal, Enrique, "Think Tanks y Partidos Políticos en América Latina", Primera Edición, agosto de 2009.

Mendizabal, Enrique, "Think Tanks in Latin America: What Are They and What Drives Them?", Foreign Affairs Latin America, 2012.

Garcé, Adolfo and Gerardo Uña, "Think Tanks and Public Policies in Latin America", Fundación Siena and CIPPEC,

Buenos Aires, Argentina, 2010.

Gerardo, Uña, "Think Tank en Argentina, Sobreviviendo a la tensión entre la participación y la permanencia", Documento de Trabajo, Noviembre de 2007.

Smith, James A. , "The Idea Brokers: Think Tanks and the Rise of the New Policy Elite", New York, The Free Press, 1993.

McGann, James G. , "Global Think Tanks", Routledge, 2010.

McGann, James G. , "Global Think Tanks", Routledge, 2011.

Arin, Kubilay Yado: Think Tanks, Springer VS, 2014.

Marshall, T. H. , "Social Policy", The 4th Edition, London: Hutchinson, 1975.

Weidenbaum, Murray, "Competition of Ideas", Transaction Publishers, New Brunswick, New Jersey.

Aste, Norma Correa, Enrique Mendizabal, "Vínculos entre conocimiento y política: el rol de la investigación en el debate public en América Latina", Primera edición, Lima, agosto de 2011.

Dickson, Paul, "Think Tank". New York: Atheneum, 1971.

Rich, Andrew and R. Kent Weaver, "Think Tanks, the Media and the Policy Process". Paper presented at the 1997 annual meeting of the American Political Science Association, Washington DC, August 1997.

Rich, Andrew, "US Think Tank and The Intersection of Ideology Advocacy and Influence", NIRA Review, Winter 2001.

Rich, Andrew, "Perceptions of Think Tanks in American Politics, A Survey of Congressional Staff and Journalists". Burson-Marstellar Worldwide Report, December 1997.

Taylor-Gooby, P. Dale, "Social Theory and Social Welfare". London: Arnold, 1981.

Zhu, Xufeng, "The Rise of Think Tanks in China", Routledge, 2013.

［日］福川伸次:《政策形成過程における日本のシンクタンクの役割》,《シンクタンクの動向 2002》,2002 年。

［日］鈴木崇弘:《日本になぜ(米国型)シンクタンクが育たなかったのか?》,《季刊政策・経営研究》,2011 年第

2 期。

［日］小池洋次:《政策形成とシンクタンク－日米比較を
　　中心に－》,《シンクタンクの動向 2002》,2002 年。

［日］小林陽太郎:《代替的政策形成機関としてのシンク
　　タ ン ク の 役 割》,《シ ン ク タ ン ク の 動 向 2003》,
　　2003 年。

Appendix

Chronicle of Events of Global Think Tank Evaluation Project

13th February, 2014	The Global Think Tank Evaluation Project Department under the Chinese Evaluation Center for Humanities and Social Sciences was established.
21st March, 2014	Discussion on thoughts and methods in the think tank evaluation process with Li Wei, researcher from the Institute of Sociology, China Academy of Social Sciences.
21st April, 2014	Discussion on statistical problems in think tank evaluation process with Zhao Yanyun, dean of School of Statistics, Renmin University.
25th April, 2014	Discussion on statistical problems in think tank evaluation process with Yang Qi, director of Department of Data Network, China Academy of Social Sciences knowing about the situation of the library's database.
10th – 17th June, 2014	Visited a number of German think tanks, including Bonn Academy of Applied Politics, German Institute of Global and Area Studies, WZB Berlin Social Science Center, Institute for Media and Communication Policy, for a better understanding of the operation situation of German think tanks.
18th July, 2014	Organized an expert seminar with the participation of 17 experts from various fields of research and discussed the rationality of the source think tanks and the feasibility of the methodology.
25th July, 2014	Discussion and exchange of views on topics like the construction of think tanks and the think tank evaluation, etc with Ge Licheng, vice-president of Zhejiang Academy of Social Sciences.
2nd September, 2014	Conference with Zhu Xufeng, professor from School of Public Policy and Administration, Tsinghua University and discussion on the construction of Chinese and foreign think tanks.
3rd September, 2014	The Global Think Tank Evaluation Project Department was renamed as Department of Institution Evaluation.
15th October, 2014	Visited Ningxia Academy of Social Sciences and had a discussion on the evaluation of academic journals and think tanks with its vice-president Zhang Shaoming.

contd.

21st – 22nd October, 2014	A pilot survey was carried out at the Institute of European Studies, CASS.
23rd October, 2014	A pilot survey was carried out at the Institute of West Asia and Africa Studies, CASS.
24th October, 2014	Pilot surveys were carried out at National Institute Of International Strategy and Institute of World Economics & International Politics, CASS.
27th October,2014	Conference at Party School of the Central Committee of CPC.
27th October,2014	Conference with American think tank expert James McGann. Both sides introduced their evaluation methods and project progress.
28th October, 2014	Pilot surveys were carried out at Institute of Russian, East European and Central Asian Studies and Institute of Japanese Studies, CASS.
30th October, 2014	A pilot survey was carried out at the Institute of Latin American Studies, CASS.
9th – 12th November, 2014	Visited Guangxi Academy of Social Sciences and Party School of CPC Guangxi Committee.
9th – 14th November, 2014	Visited Taiwan Research Institute, Research Center of The Macro Economy, Center for Accounting Studies, Center for Southeast Asian Studies of Xiamen University and Fujian Academy of Social Sciences.
3rd December,2014	Visited Brookings-Tsinghua Center for Public Policy.
10th December, 2014	Organized a seminar and discussed with domestic think tank research experts regarding the definition and methodology of think tank evaluation.
11th December, 2014	Reception of the delegation of National Research Council for Economics, Humanities and Social Sciences and conference with representatives from 14 South Korean government—funded think tanks.
20th December, 2014	Exchange of views with Ji Lianggang, president of Hebei University of Economics and Business and Zhang Xiaoping, director of Hebei Academy of Social Sciences, etc regarding the evaluation of academic journals and think tanks.
22nd – 26th December, 2014	Visited Xinjiang Academy of Social Sciences, Xinjiang Normal University, Party School of Xinjiang Autonomous Region, and Xinjiang Production and Construction Corps.
26th December, 2014	Attended the inauguration ceremony of E-commerce Research Institute, University of Shanghai for Science and Technology.

contd.

28th − 31st December, 2014	Visited Qinghai Academy of Social Sciences, Qinghai Provincial Party School and Qinghai Institute of Socialism.
5th January, 2015	Visited National Academy of Economic Strategy, Institute for Urban and Environmental Studies, Institute of Finance and Banking, Institute of Population and Labor Economics of CASS and learned about the operation situation of these institutes for economic studies.
6th January, 2015	Meeting with Xu Heping, former director the Office of Ministry of Science and Technology.
7th January, 2015	Reception of the delegation of China Development Research Institute led by its secretary-general Mou Shanrong. Had an in-depth understanding of its development history, the ways and contents of work as a think tank.
12th − 16th January, 2015	Visited Anhui Academy of Social Sciences and Party School of Anhui Province.
21st − 23rd January, 2015	Attended the Annual Conference of Institutes for International Studies of CASS and communicated with experts on think tank evaluation project.
23rd − 28th February, 2015	Visited the United States and shared views with experts from ten think tanks, including Council on Foreign Relations, NYU Center for International Cooperation, Brookings Institution, Heritage Foundation, Carnegie Endowment for International Peace, American Enterprise Institute, World Resources Institute, Institute of Strategic and International Studies, Urban Institute and Cato Institute, having a better understanding of the development and operation situation of major think tank in the US.
13th − 14th March, 2015	Visited Henan Academy of Social Sciences and discussion conference with the president, Yu Xin'an, in which he introduced the efforts that the academy had been making in the construction of think tanks and in trying to provide intelligence support for local economic and social development.
16th March, 2015	Reception of delegation of Academy of Military Sciences PLA China and discussion on the evaluation of scientific research products and think tanks.
17th March, 2015	Visited Institute of Russian, East European and Central Asian Studies, Institute of West Asia and Africa Studies, National Institute Of International Strategy of CASS to learn about think tanks in these regions and to discuss cooperation in acquiring datas.
23rd March, 2015	Visited the Institute of European Studies, CASS.

contd.

25th March, 2015	Visited National School of Development at Pekin University and had a conference with the vice-president Huang Yiping.
2nd April, 2015	Visited Brookings-Tsinghua Center for Public Policy and had a conference with its director Prof. Qi Ye.
12th April, 2015	Conference with the president of Zhejiang Gongshang University regarding the construction and evaluation of think tanks.
16th April, 2015	Visited China Institute of International Studies and had a discussion conference with its vice-president Guo Xiangang.
21st April, 2015	Visited Institute of American Studies, CASS and had a conference with the director Zheng Bingwen, directors of different research departments and other experts regarding the characteristics of American think tanks and the methods used in the think tank evaluation project of McGann.
22nd April, 2015	Visited Chongyang Institute of Financial Studies of Renmin University and had a meeting with Hu Haibin, editor in chief of the Information Center, and Liu Ying, director of Research Cooperation Department to have a deeper understanding of RDCY's operation situation.
23rd April, 2015	Visited China Institute of Contemporary International Relations and had a meeting with the president Ji Zhiye and directors of different departments.
28th April, 2015	Visited China Center for International Economic Exchanges and had a discussion conference with Xu Hongcai, director of Economic Research Division.
30th April, 2015	Visited Chinese Academy of Governance and had a meeting with Chen Bingcai, deputy director of Training Department, and Niu Xianzhong, deputy director of General Office.
6th May, 2015	Visited Horizon Research Consultancy Group. Had a conference with Guo Weiwei, research director of International Development Institute, Zhang Hui, general manager and Jiang Jianjian, deputy general manager and learned about the evaluation system and methods of its China Think Tank Impact Report.
22nd May, 2015	Visited Party School of the Central Committee of CPC and had a meeting with professors from School of Economics and School of Training to discuss think tank evaluation issues.
15th May, 2015	The office of Institution Evaluation Department was moved to the Archives Building of CASS.

contd.

30th May – 6th June, 2015	Visited State Innovative Institute for Public Management and Policy Studies, Center for Contemporary Marxism in Foreign Countries, Center for American Studies, Center for Japanese Studies, Institute of World Economy, Information and Communication Research Center, China Center for Economic Studies, Center for Comparative Studies of Modernization at Fudan University; Center for Russian Studies, Institute of Schooling Reform and Development, Chinese Modern Thought and Culture Research Institute at East China Normal University; Institute of Accounting and Finance at Shanghai University of Finance and Economics; Center for Russian Studies, Center for European Union Studies, Centre for British Studies, Center for Middle East Studies at Shanghai International Studies University; German Academic Center , UNEP-Tongji Institute of Environment for Sustainable Development at Tongji University; Shanghai Institute for International Studies; Shanghai Party Institute of CCP & Shanghai Administration Institute ; Shanghai Academy of Social Sciences; Shanghai Huaxia Social Development Research Institute and CEIBS Lujiazui International Finance Research Center.
1st June, 2015	Published an article *Small and professional rather than large and comprehensive: how to build professional think tanks with Chinese characteristics* in China Youth Daily.
4th June,2015	Attended the 34th Contemporary Think Tank Forum.
12th June, 2015	Participated in the "Think Tank Interview" held by Hexun. com, which recorded an interview " Where is the road to the construction of Chinese think tanks?".
17th – 23rd June, 2015	Visited several major think tanks in UK and Belgium, including the Chatham House, China Institute of SOAS University of London, Centre for European Reform, EU40, Bruegel, Friends of Europe, European Centre for International Political Economy, International Crisis Group, Egmont Royal Institute for International Relations for a better understanding of the operation situation of European think tanks.
23rd June, 2015	Published an article *Cold Thinking on Think Tank Heat* in People's Daily.
30th June,2015	Attended the China-South Korea Humanities Exchange Policy Forum.
2nd July, 2015	Visited Development Research Center of the State Council and had a discussion meeting with Lai Youwei, deputy director of General Office, and Liu Lihui, head of Department of General Affairs.

contd.

8th July, 2015	Published an article *The Japanese think tanks, which swing between commercial interests and public responsibility* in China. org.
10th – 13th July, 2015	Visited Research Institute of Economy, Trade & Industry, (Japan) and Daiwa Institute of Research Ltd. (Japan) had a conference with experts regarding the development course, the current situation and the future construction of Japanese think tanks.
13th July, 2015	Attended the conference *International Studies and the Construction of Think Tanks*.
14th July, 2015	Published an article *The Think Tank Rankings* in Economy & Nation Weekly.
17th July, 2015	Published an article *From "Think Tank" to "Do Tank"* in China. org.
20th July, 2015	Discussion with Qiao Jun, vice-president of Nanjing University of Finance and Economics, Ye Nanke, president of Association of Social Sciences of Nanjing, president and Party secretary of Nanjing Academy of Social Sciences and Li Chenghua, vice-president of Nanjing Academy of Social Sciences, exchanging ideas on the construction and the evaluation of think tanks.
22nd July, 2015	Published an article *Three Major Challenges Should be overcome for the Construction of Chinese Think Tanks* in Guang Ming Daily.
30th July, 2015	Attended the 2015 Think Tank Summit—Global Governance and Open Economy.
6th August, 2015	Attended the colloquium by Naoyuki Yoshino, dean of Asian Development Bank Institute.
6th August, 2015	Discussion with Jiang Lijun, Party secretary of Anhui University of Finance and Economy and Zhu Shiqun, Party secretary, president of Anhui Academy of Social Sciences on issues like the construction of think tanks and so on.
11th August, 2015	Published an article Exploit the Advantages of Think Tanks to the full in Public Diplomacy in Chinese Social Sciences Today.
25th August, 2015	Attended the CASS Forum "One Belt, One Road" and BCIM Regional Interconnection".
6th September, 2015	Visited Liao Wang Institution and had a conference with its president Wu Liang and the editor Wang Fang.
16th September, 2015	Conference with Shen Danyang, spokesman for the Ministry of Commerce and director of Research Department and discussion on think tank issues.

contd.

29th September, 2015	Reception of the delegation of Guizhou Social Sciences Association led by the Party secretary and vice-president Bao Yunkun and discussion on the construction of local think tanks.
19th October, 2015	Reception of the delegation of Shandong Social Sciences Association led by the deputy secretary of the Party and vice-president Zhou Zhonggao and discussion on the evaluation of think tanks and academic journals.
20th October, 2015	Conference with the delegation of Shanghai Academy of Social Sciences.
21st October, 2015	Conference with Gu Xueming, Chinese Academy of International Trade and Economic Cooperation, MOFCOM and discussion on the construction of new type of think tanks with Chinese characteristics and other topics.
24th – 25th October, 2015	Exchange of ideas on the evaluation of think tanks with over 10 presidents from universities of finance and economy.
30th October, 2015	Conference with Rohinton Medhora, president of Centre for International Governance Innovation.
10th November, 2015	The Second Summit of National Humanities and Social Sciences Evaluation was held in Beijing with the announcement of the global think tank rankings. More than 100 think tank experts from China, the United States, Germany, Republic of Korea, Japan, Azerbaijan, etc attended the summit for discussion on think tank issues.
12th November, 2015	Conference with Adrian Phua, vice-president of Alumni Association of S. Rajaratnam School of International Studies, Nanyang Technological University.